Sweet 16
40 Kaleidoscopes to Color
Based on Sixteens

by
Dee Faire

Also by Dee Faire

8 Ways from Sunday: 40 Kaliedoscopes to Color based on Eights

Welcome!

Ah, sweet sixteen. That strange threshold year of the young. All the wonders of the eights taken twice. Or the wonders of four (four seasons, four states of matter, four cardinal directions) squared.

A few things you might want to take note of:

● I've tried to roughly arrange the designs by complexity, with the simpler ones in front and more complex ones later, so you can have an idea of where to look depending on how ambitious you are. There're a few meticulous ones in the back.

● Don't be afraid of a lot of lines. Nobody says one area can't be the exact same color as the area next to it. Leaving an area white is also perfectly valid, especially if the point of your chosen scribble stick is bigger than it is.

● Sometimes markers and pens can bleed through, especially if you're like me and want good, saturated color. Keep some indifferent paper between the page you're working on and the next one to avoid accidental "pre-coloring" of the next page.

● If you'd like to remove a page and show it to the world (or would rather color it without having to hold the book open), one of the simplest and most reliable ways is to take a length of cotton string/fine yarn long enough that you can hold it comfortably with the spine-length of the book between them, wet it (not dripping wet, but fairly damp), then lay the book on a firm surface and open it to the page you want. Slide the cotton in against the spine. Close the book and press down on the spine for a few seconds. This will force the water into a narrow strip of the page, weakening it so you can easily tear it without worrying that it will rip out of control and go through the design. (Yes, the page above it will get wet,too, but if you don't pull at it, it will soon dry and return to its original strength.)

● These designs have been cropped to 8" x 10", a common size for frames and mattes, If you'd like to put your work on the wall, most kaleidoscopes will look their best with black mattes (especially if you're using primary colors, like those that come in eight-packs of markers). If you have a lot of earthy tones (browns and tans), you might want an off-white or beige matte.

I hope you have as much fun coloring these pages as I had making them!

Dee Faire

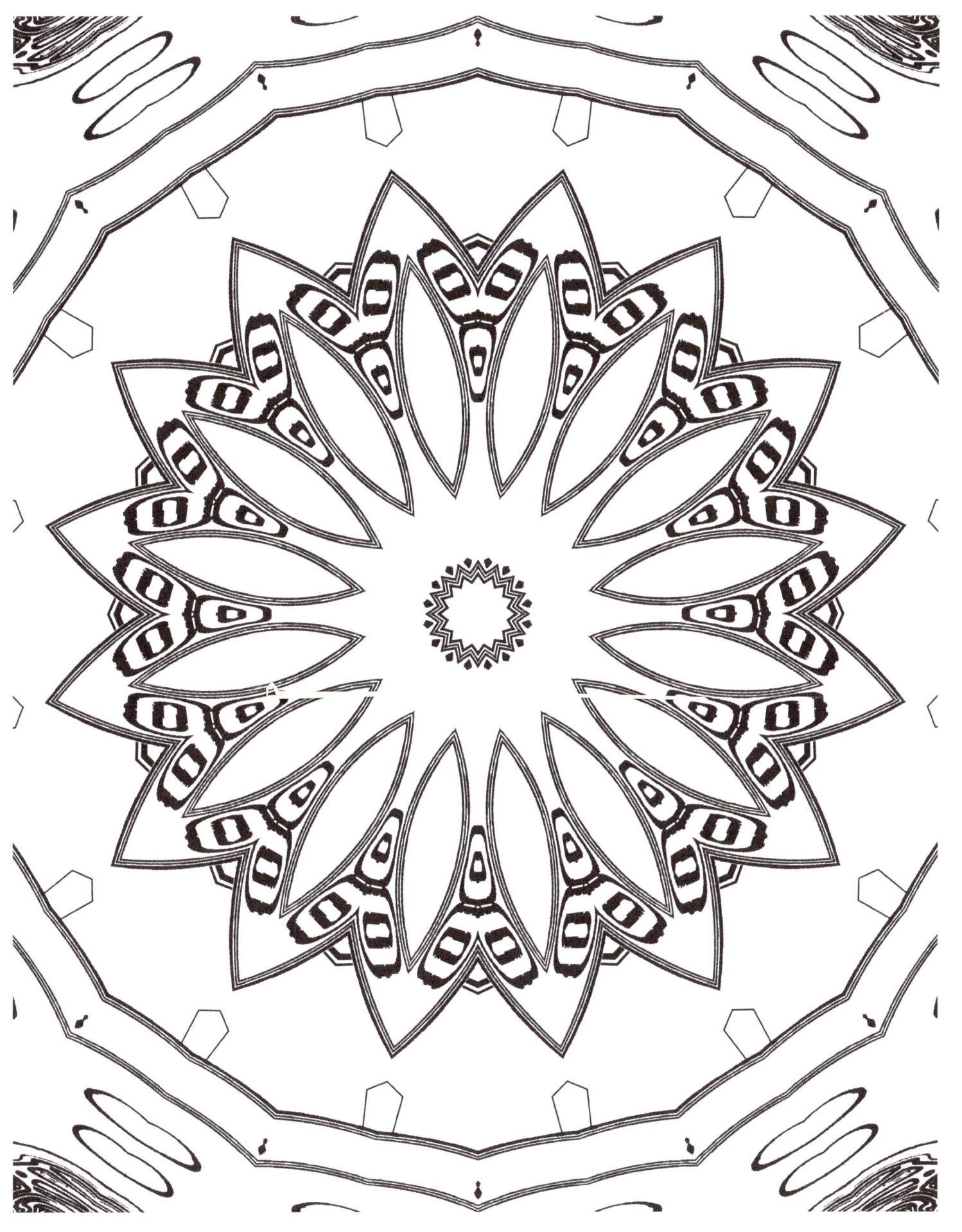

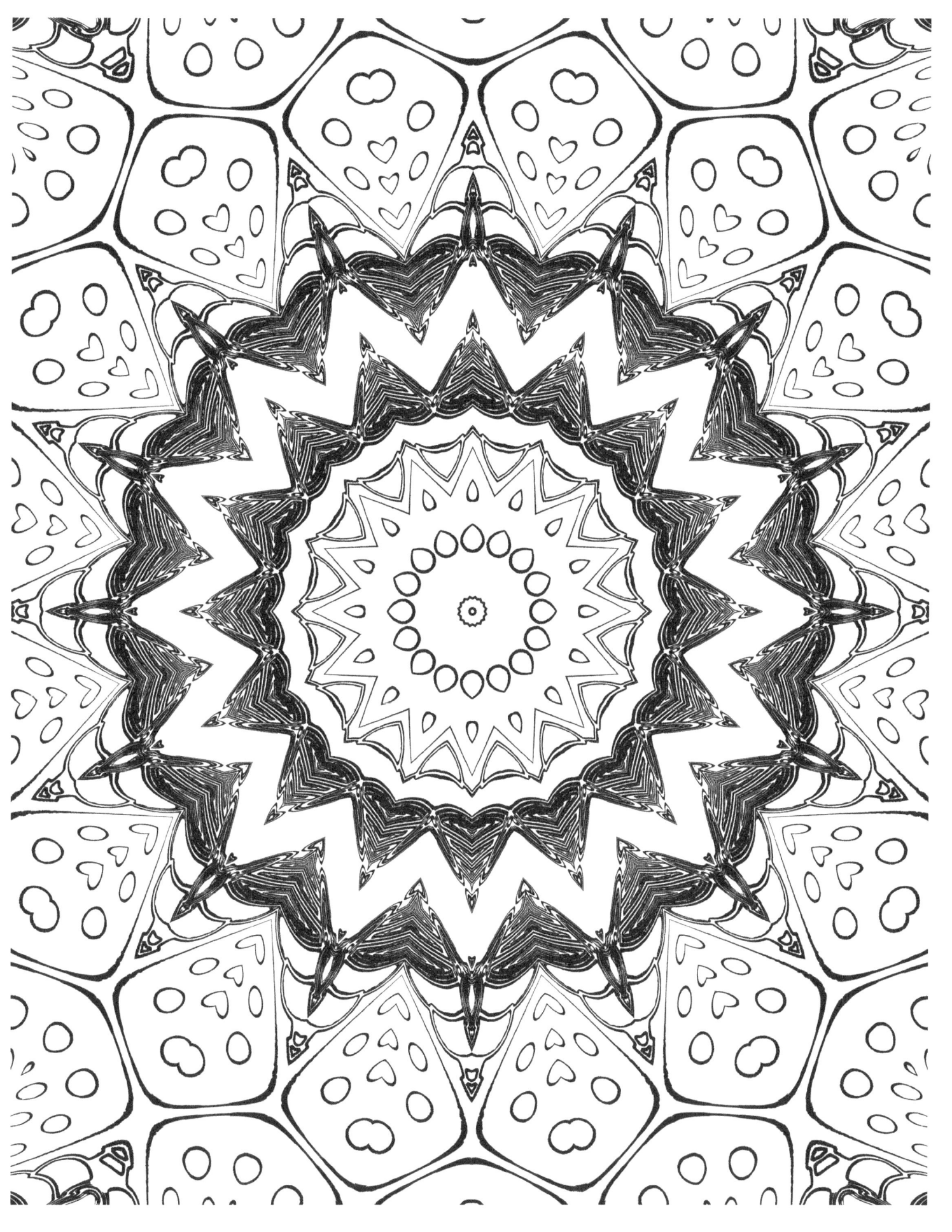

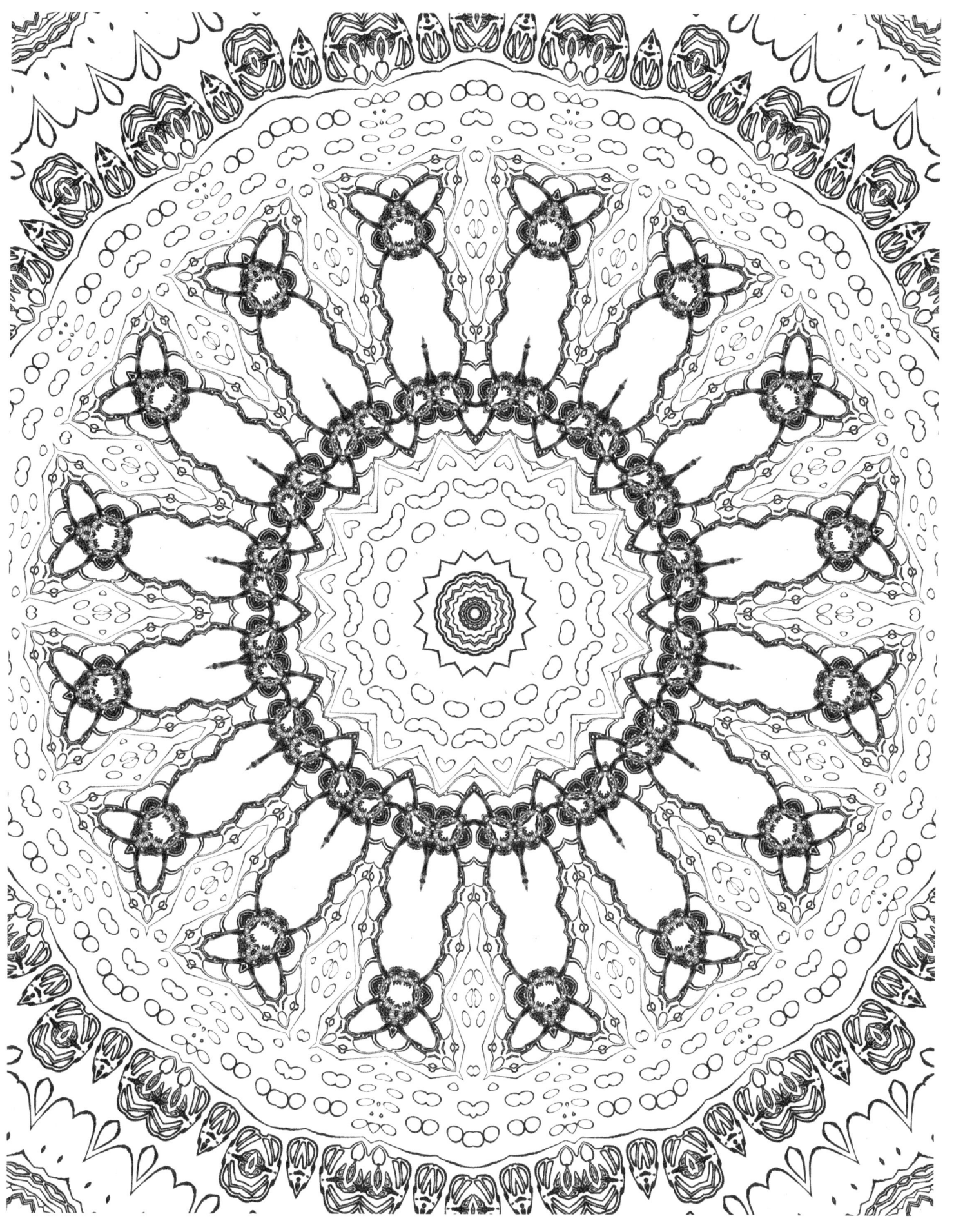

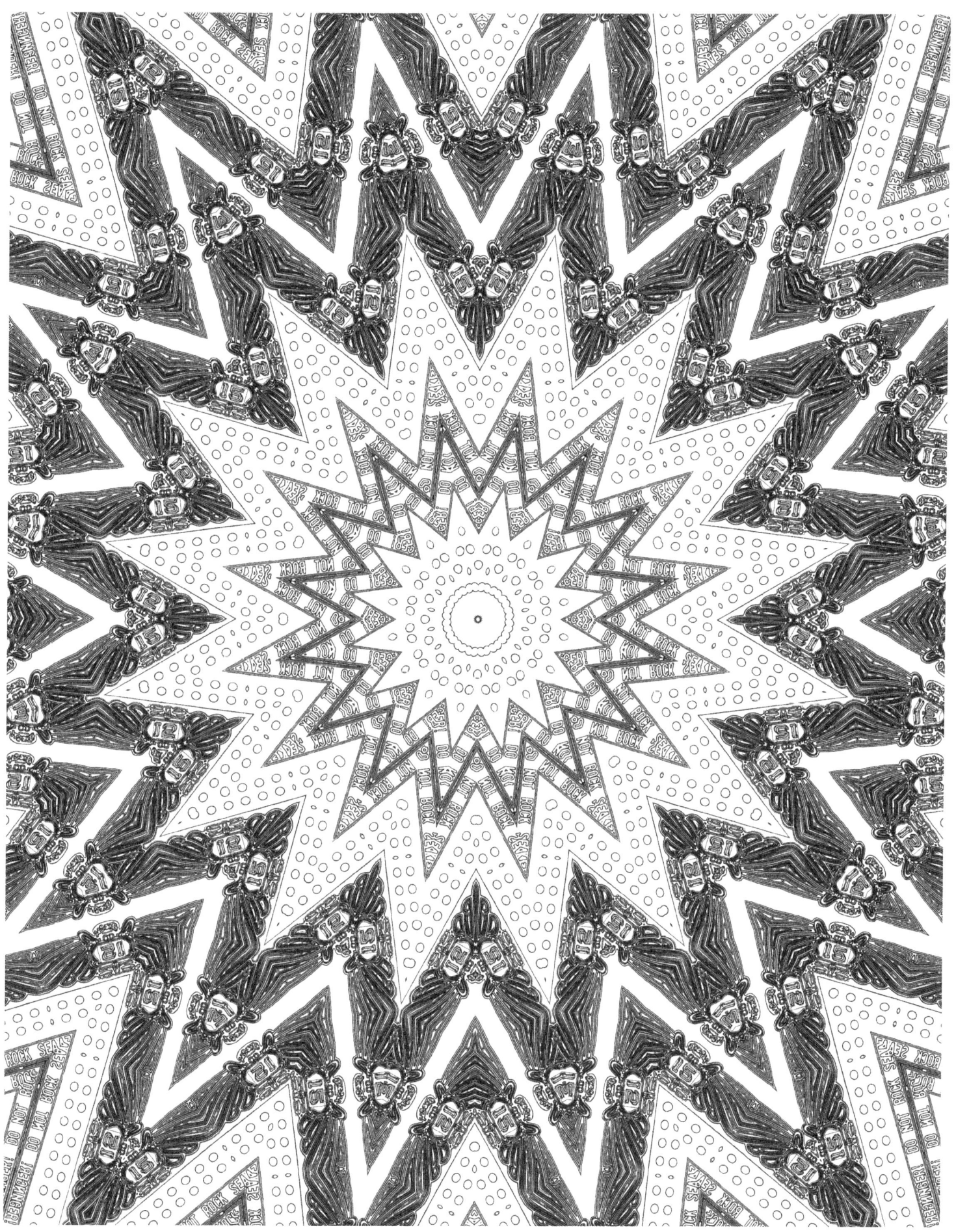

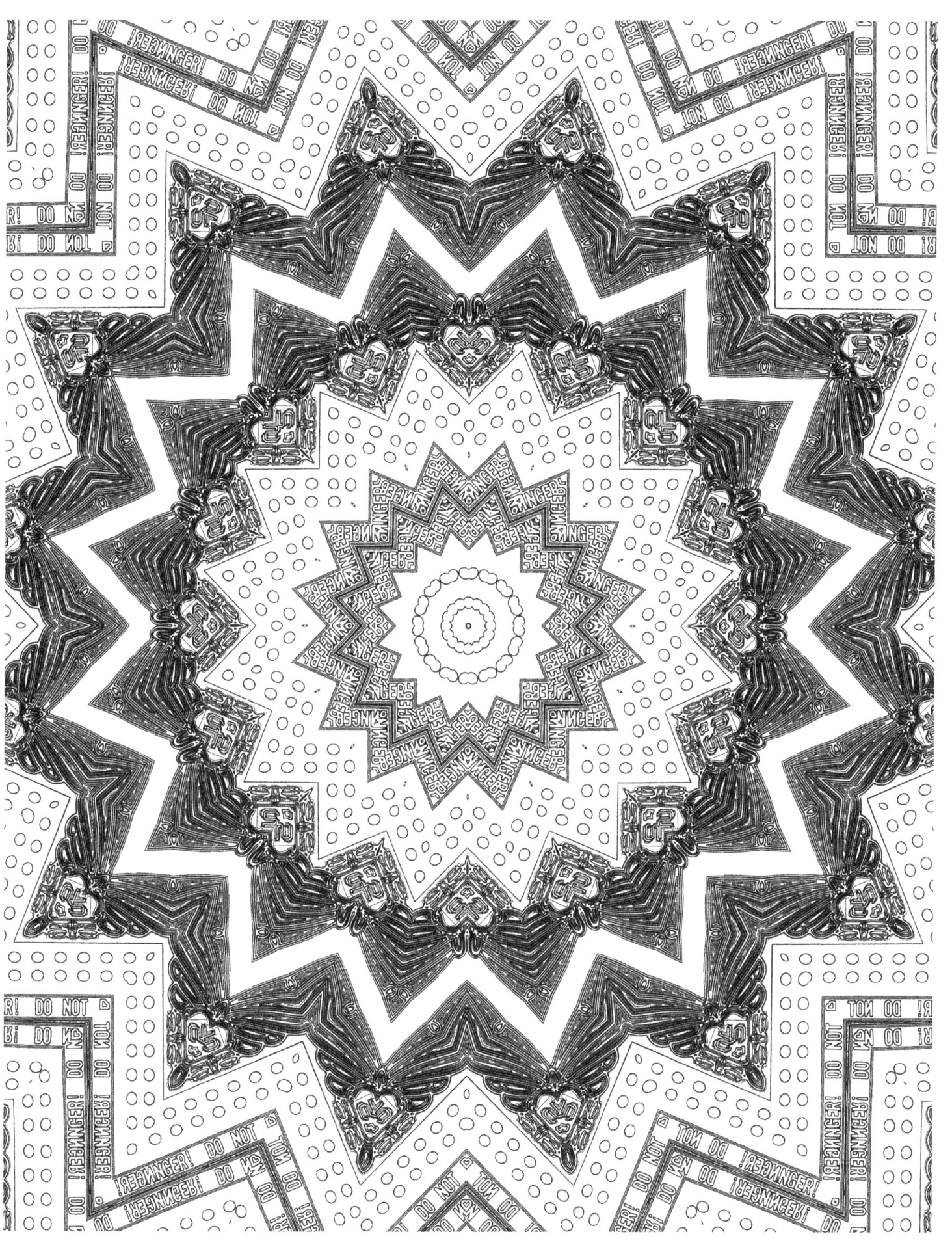

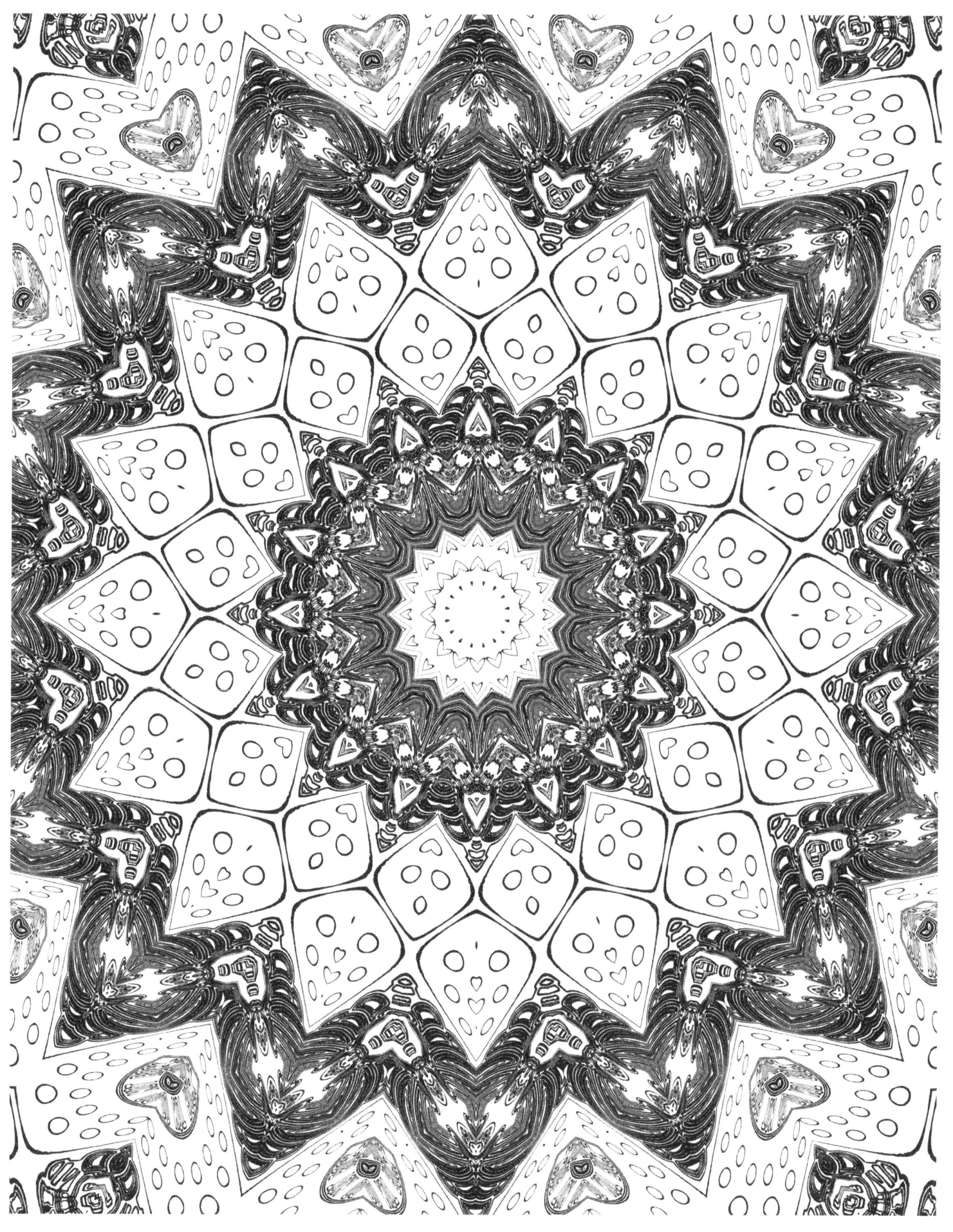

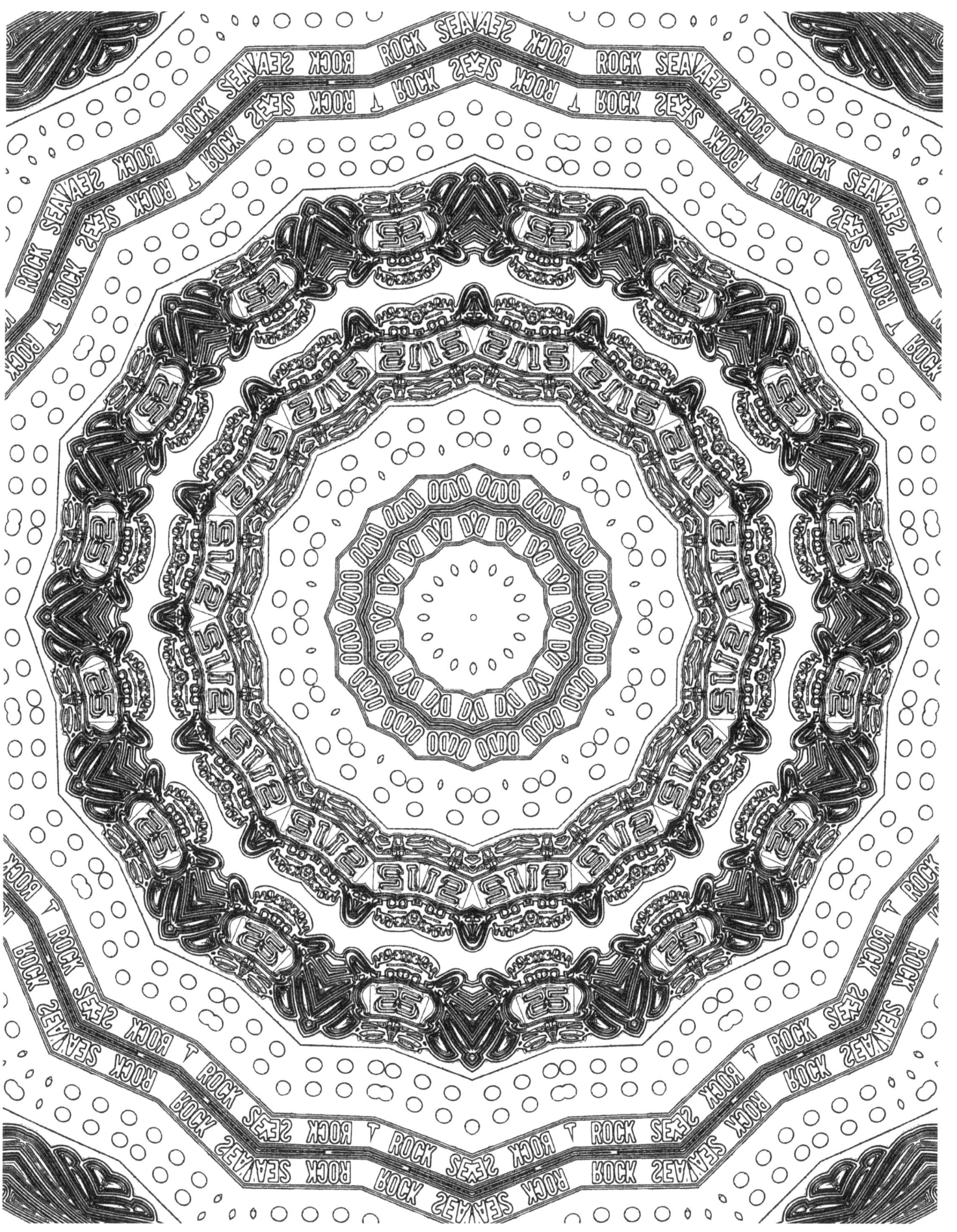

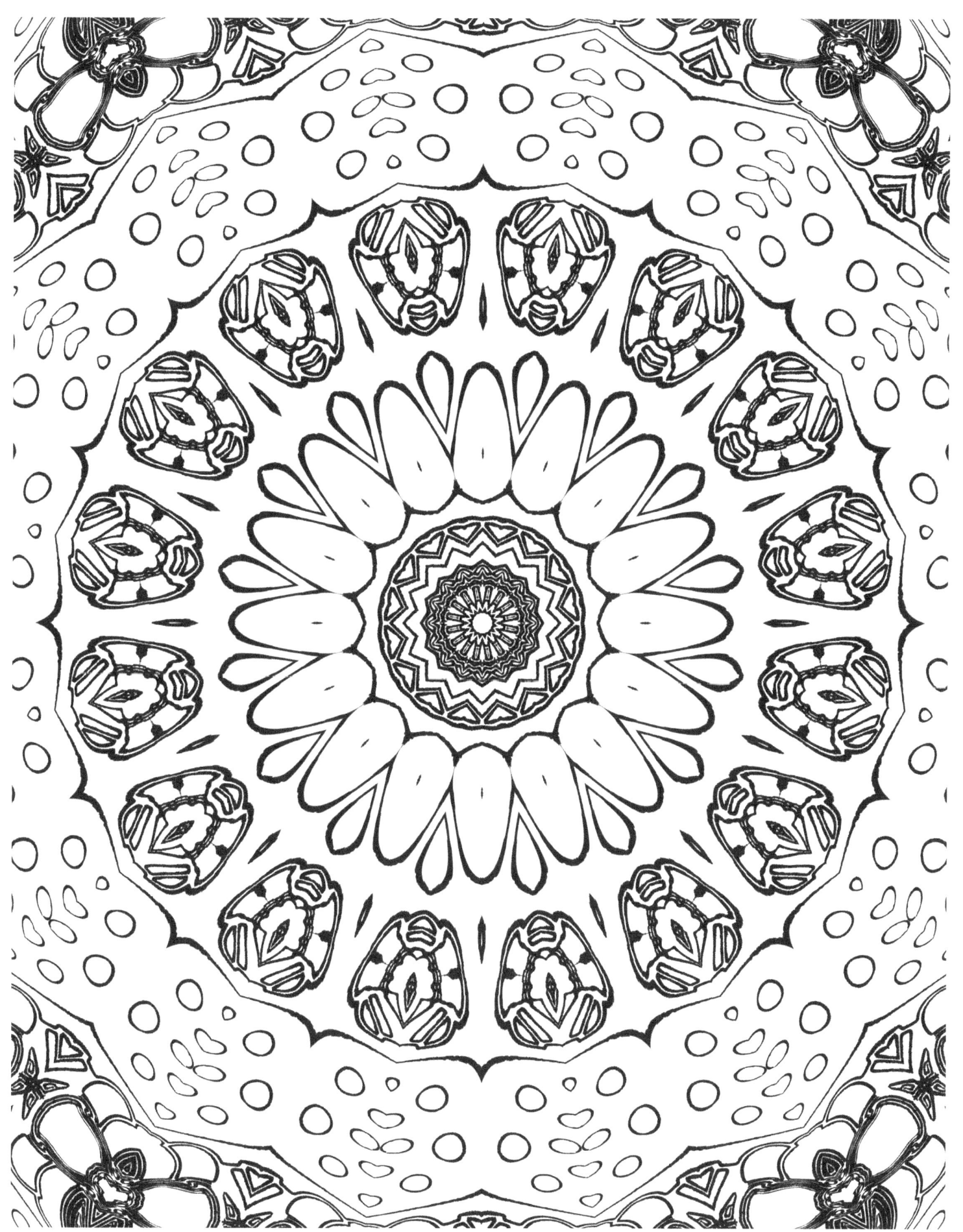

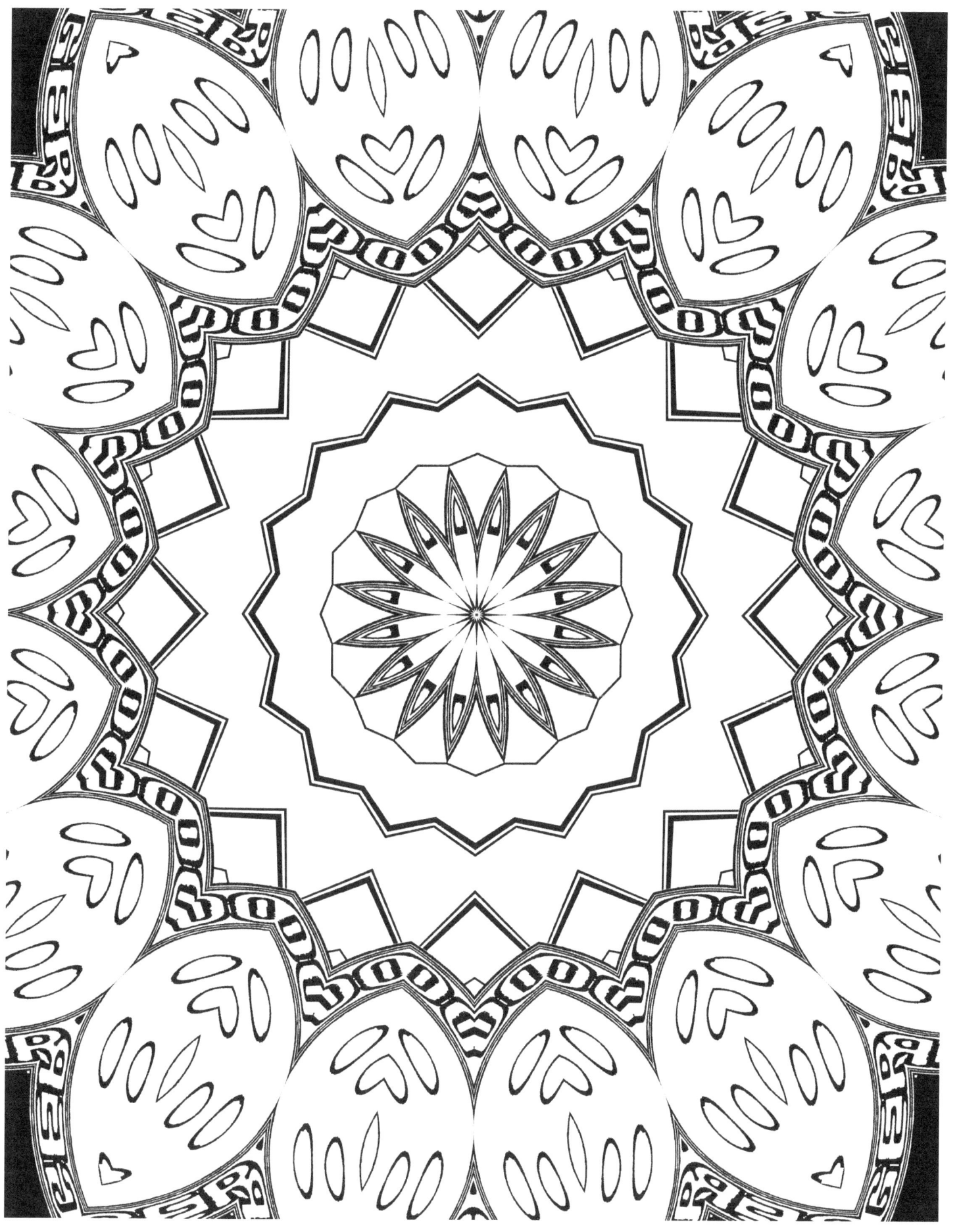

.

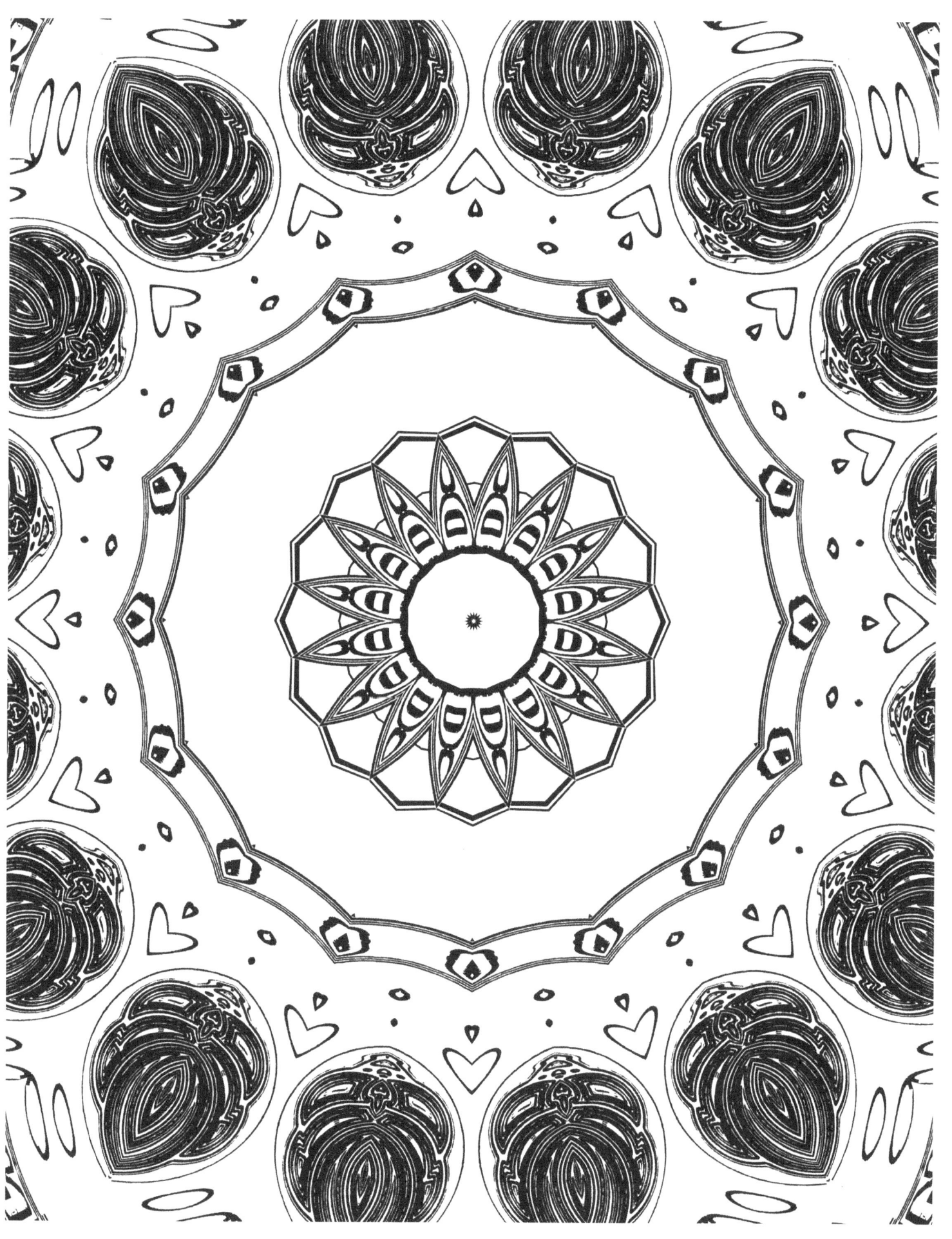

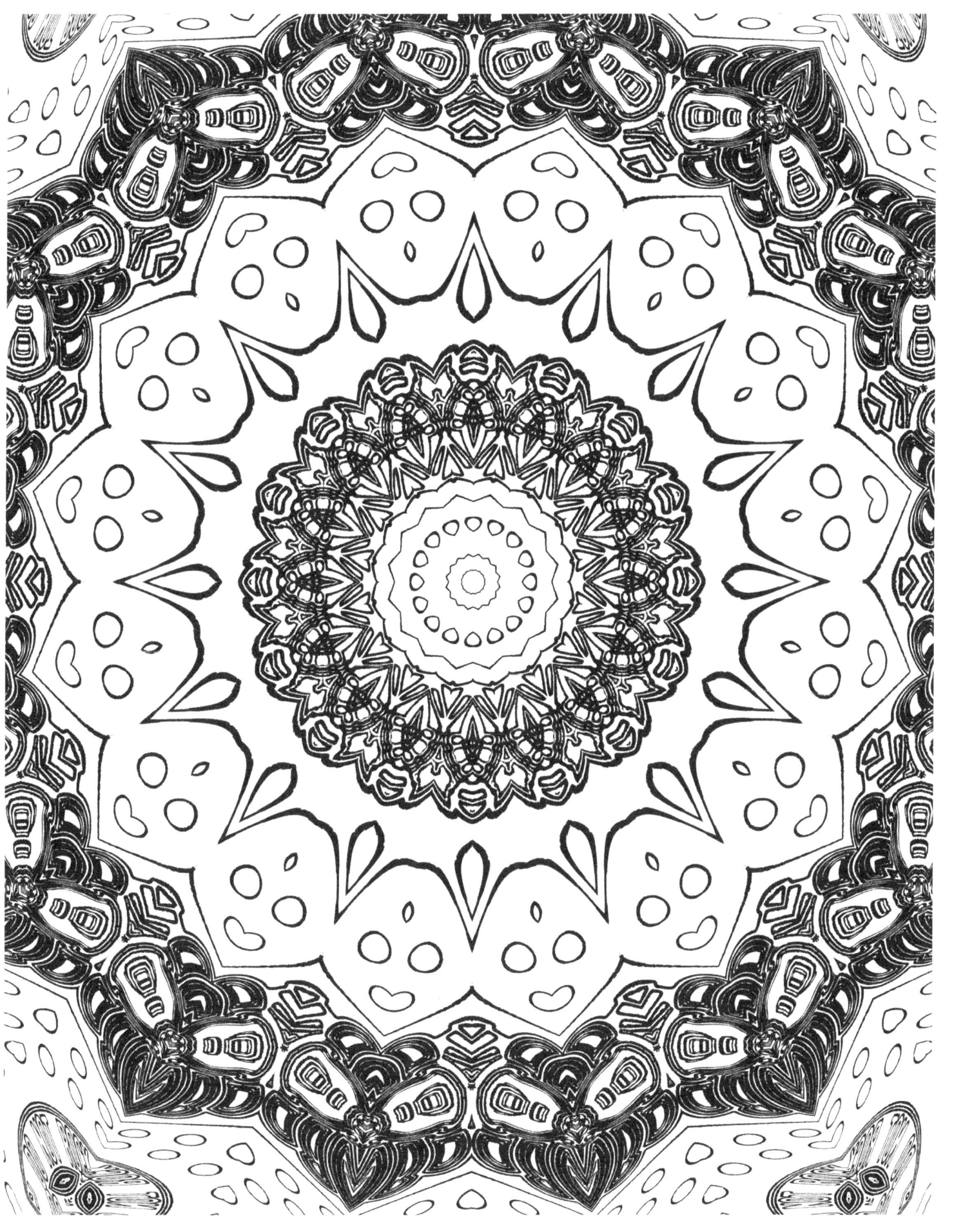

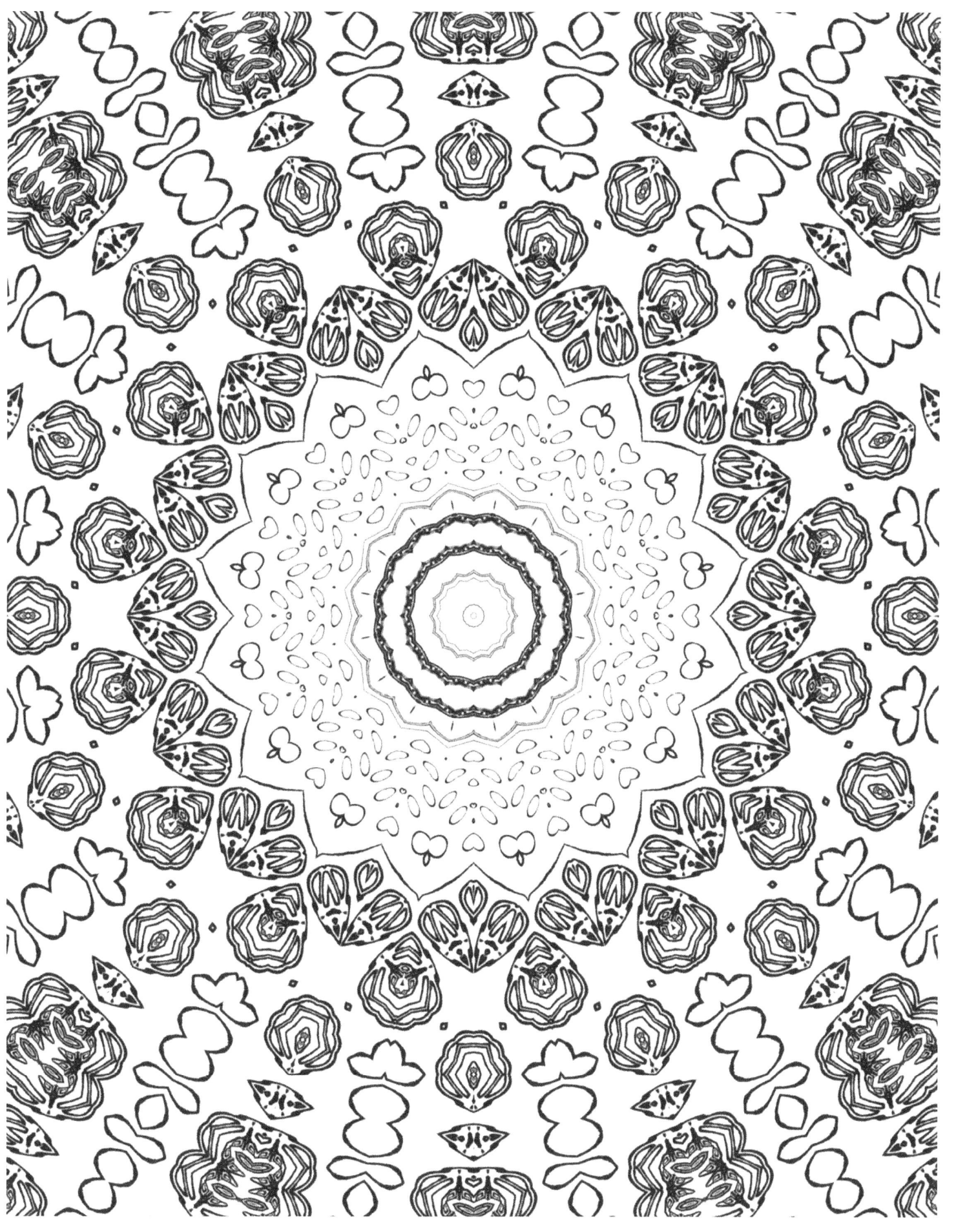

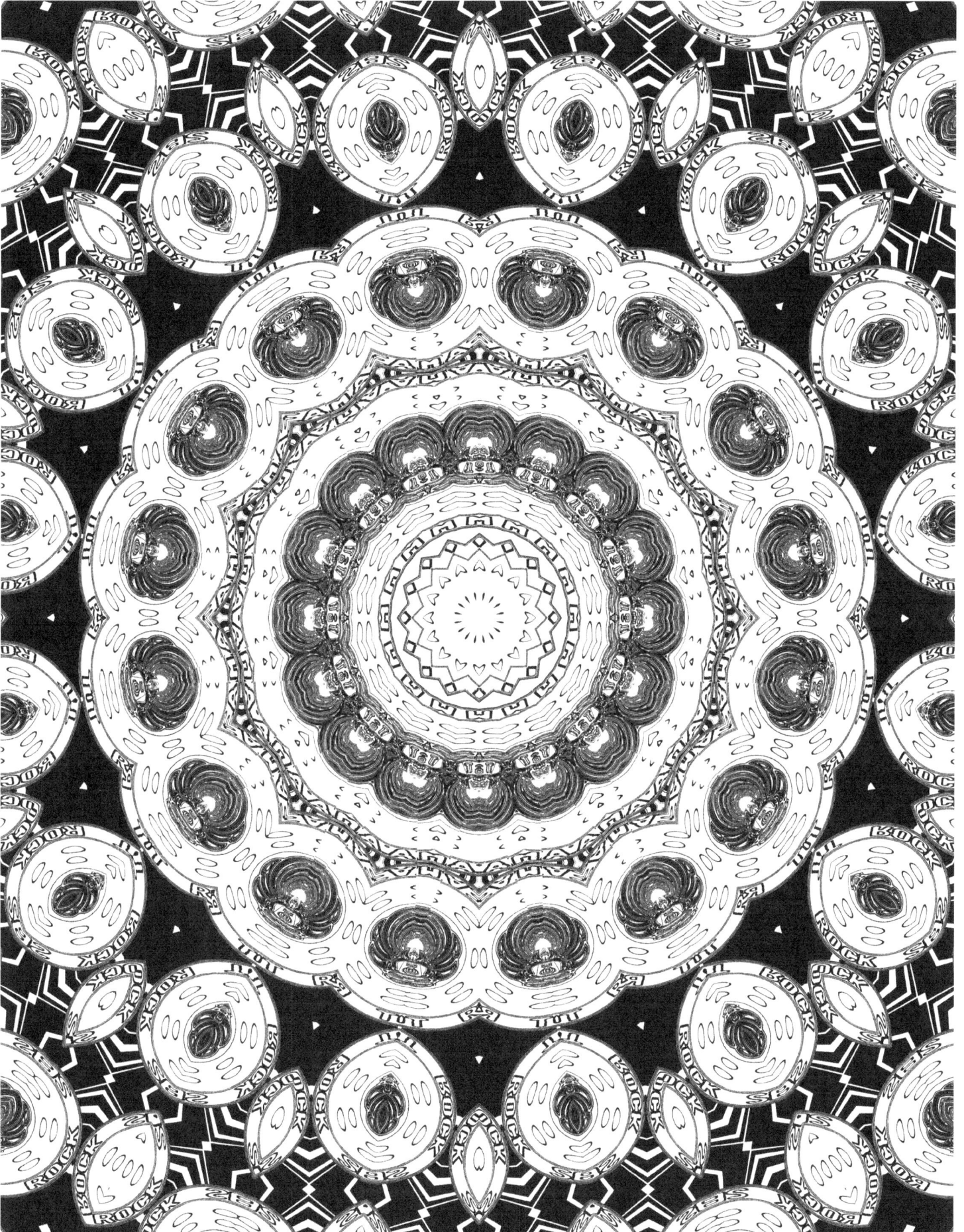

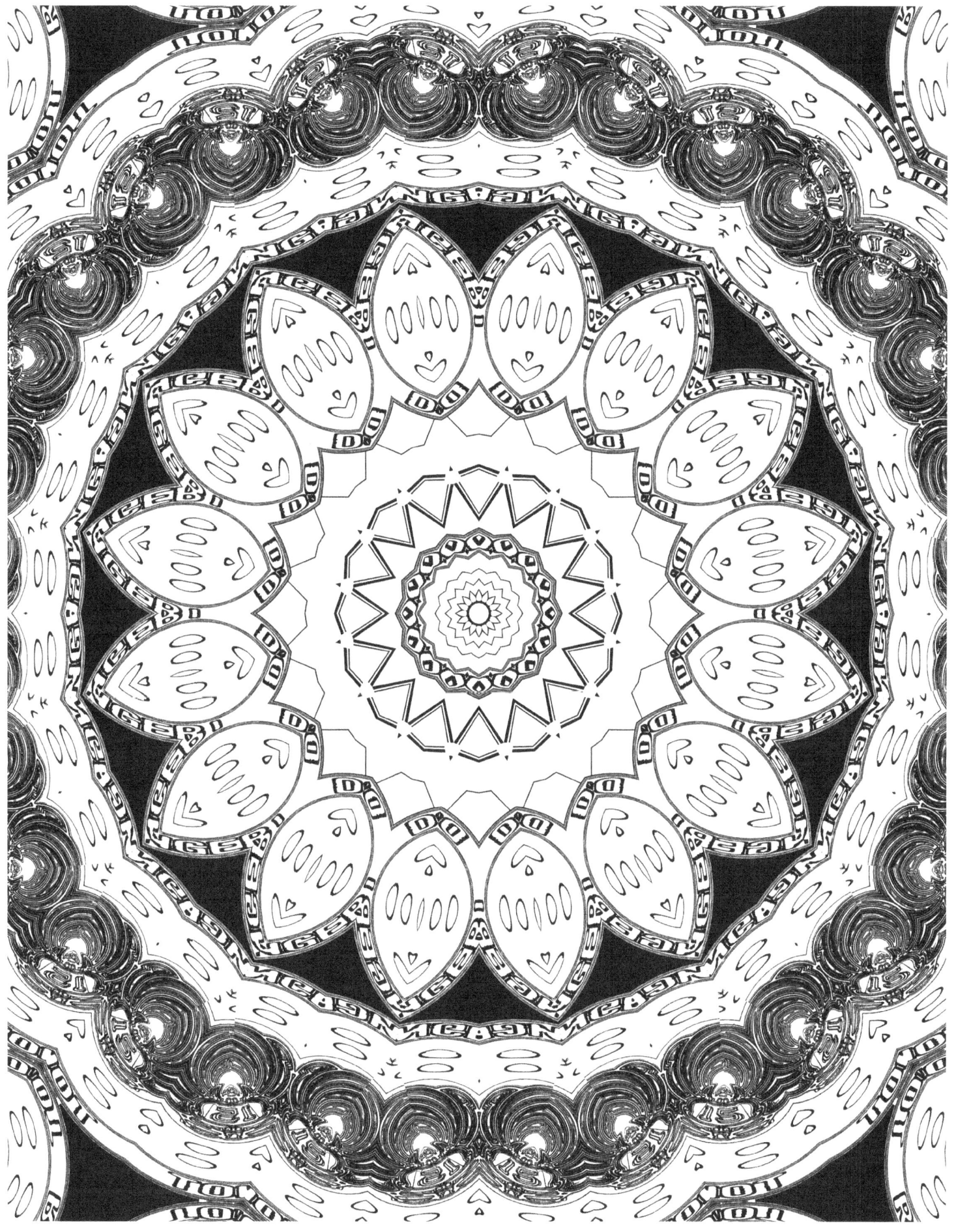

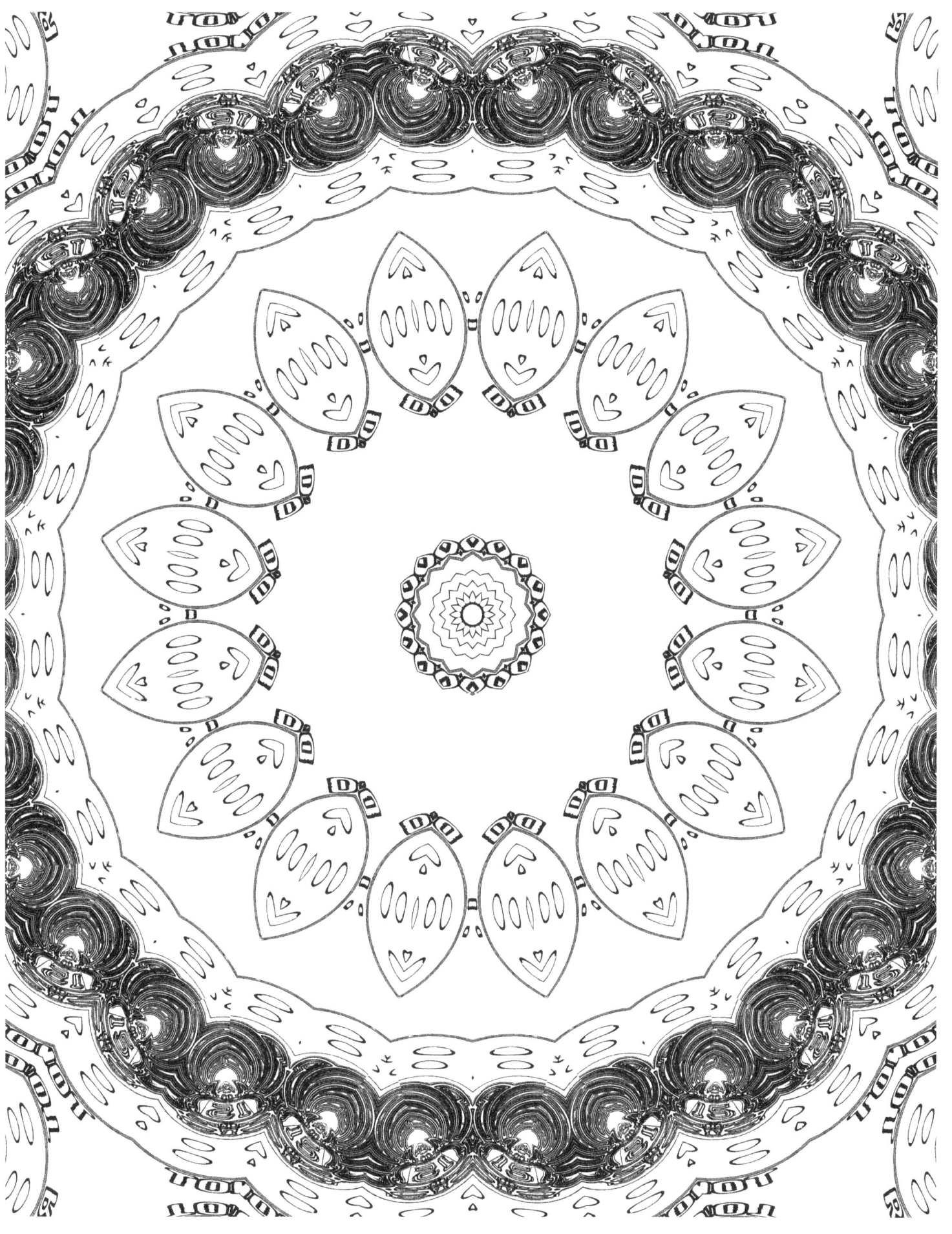

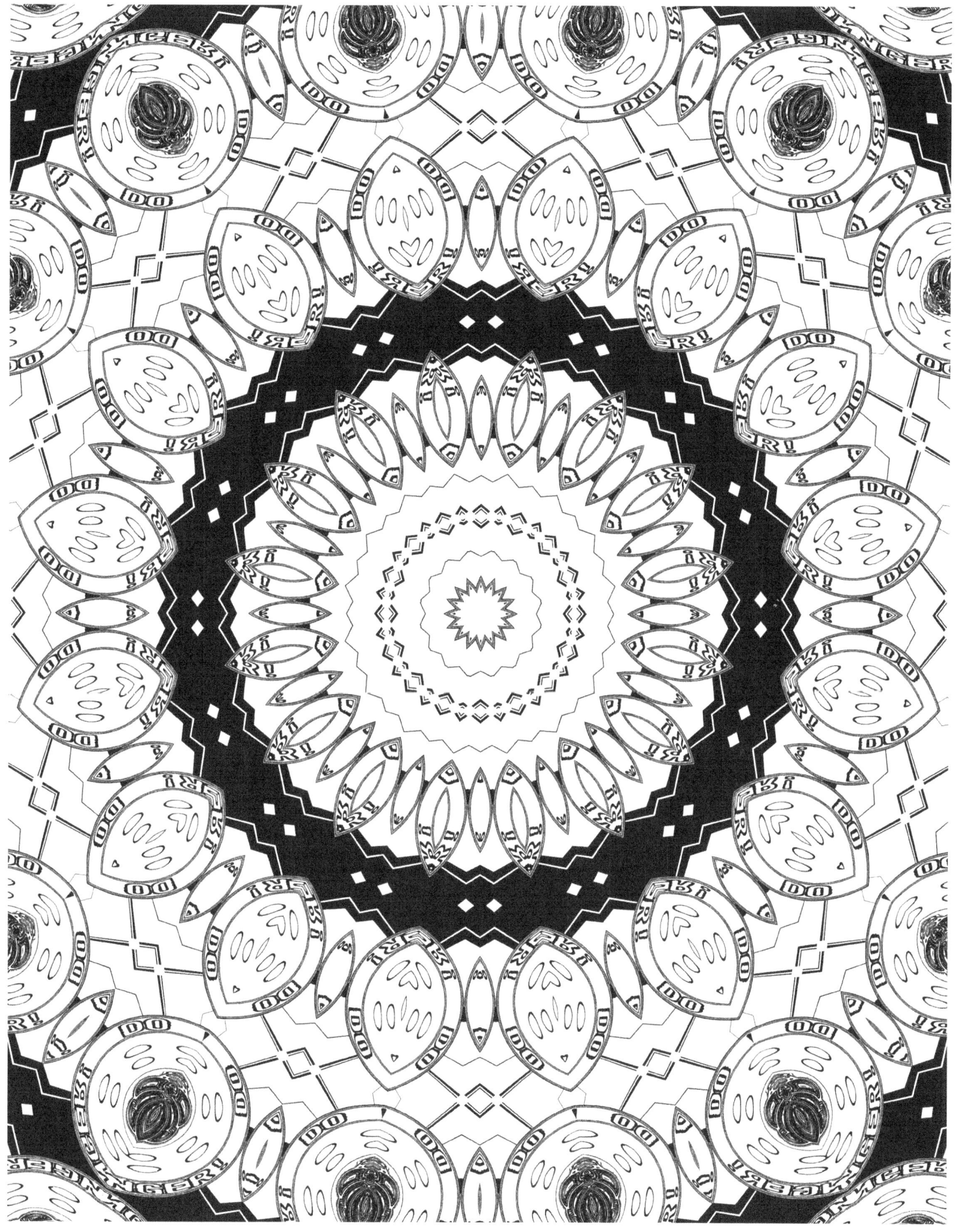

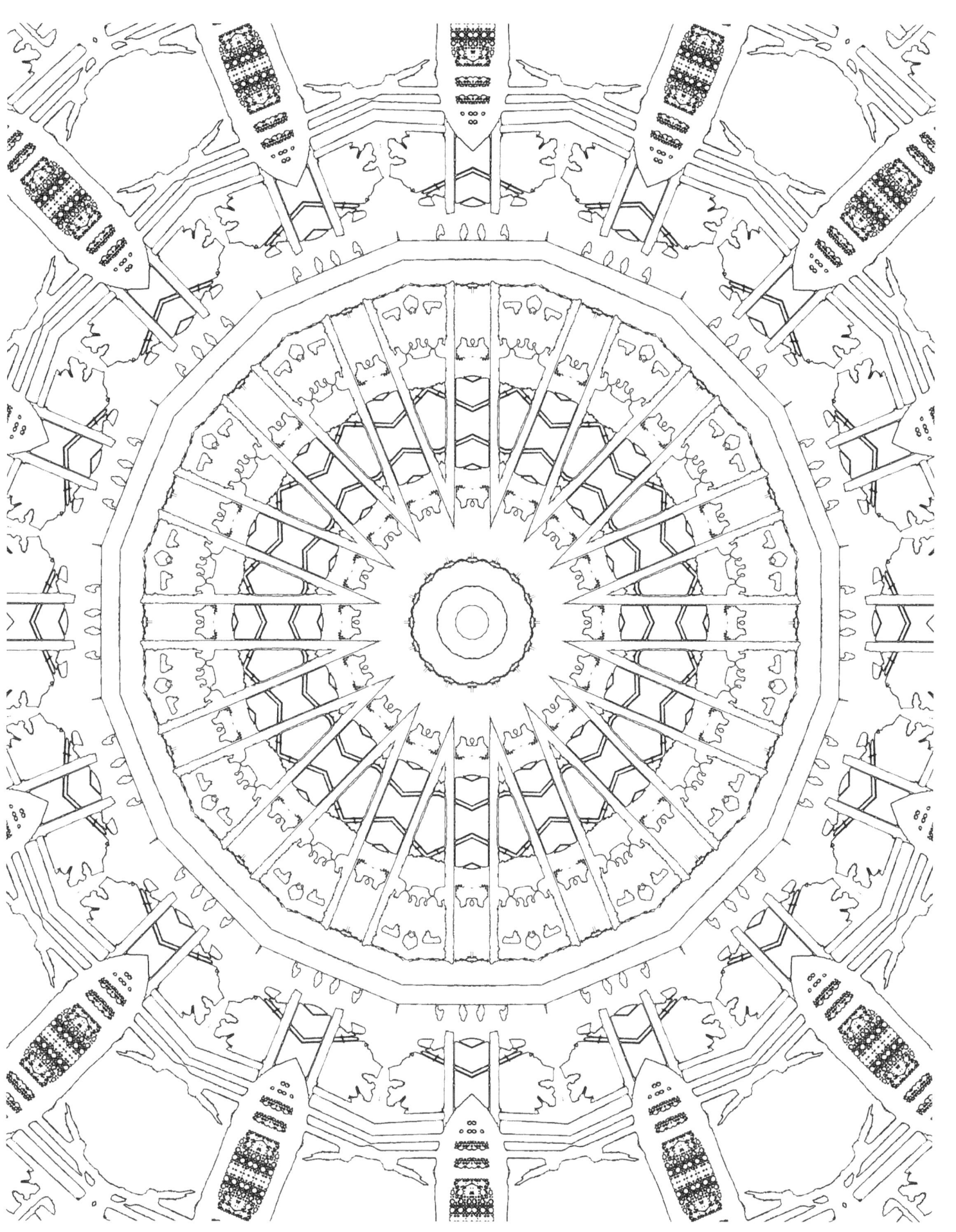

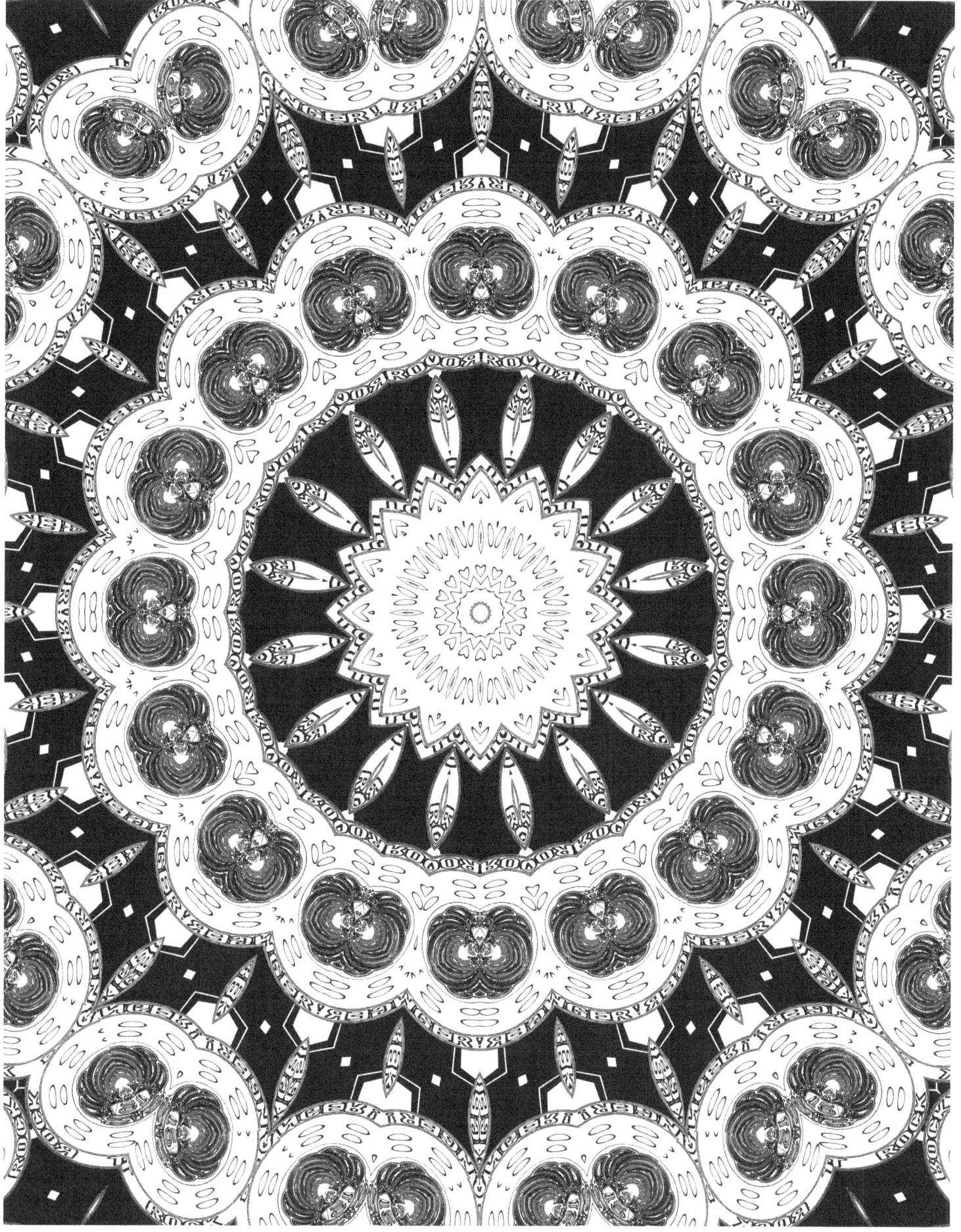

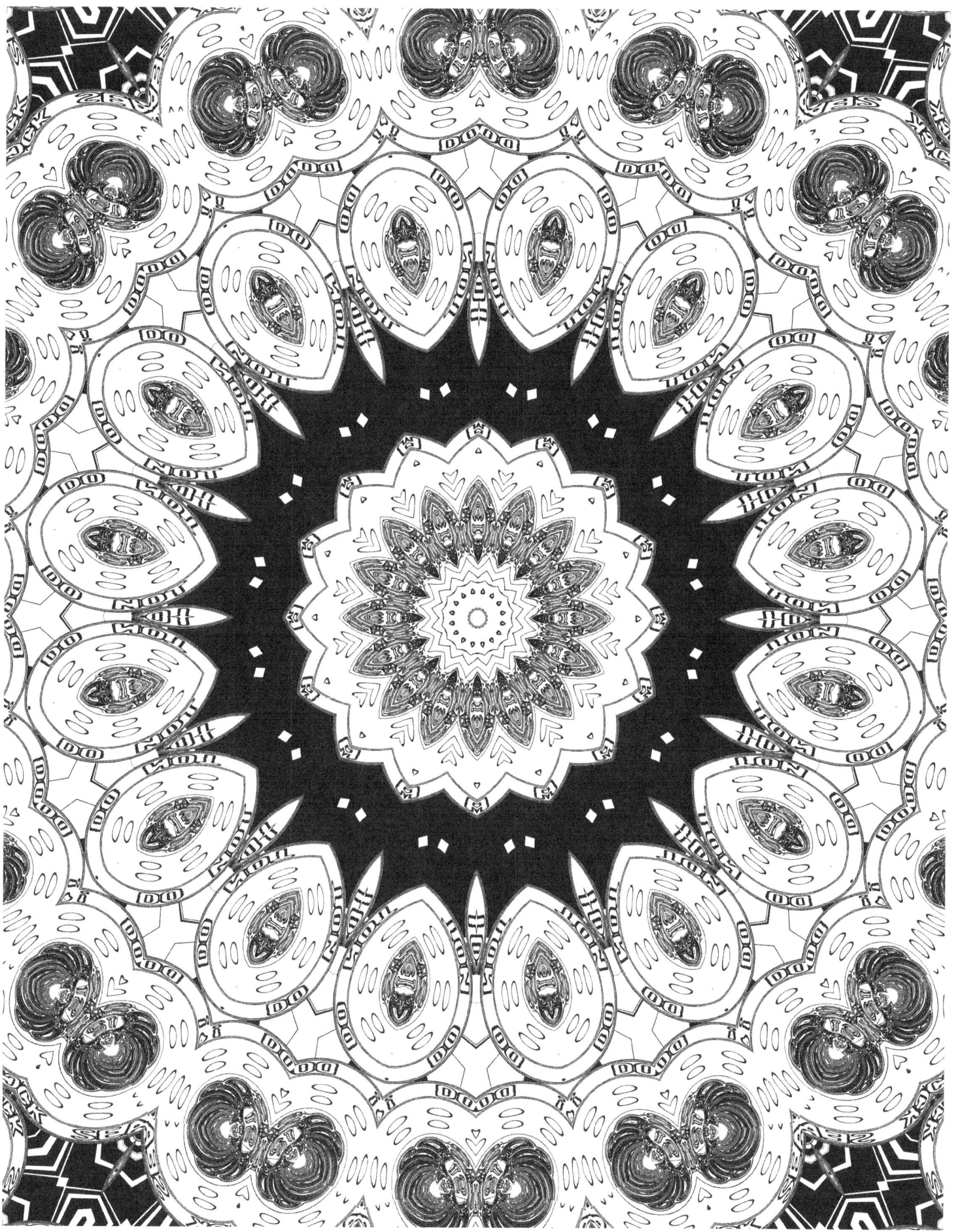

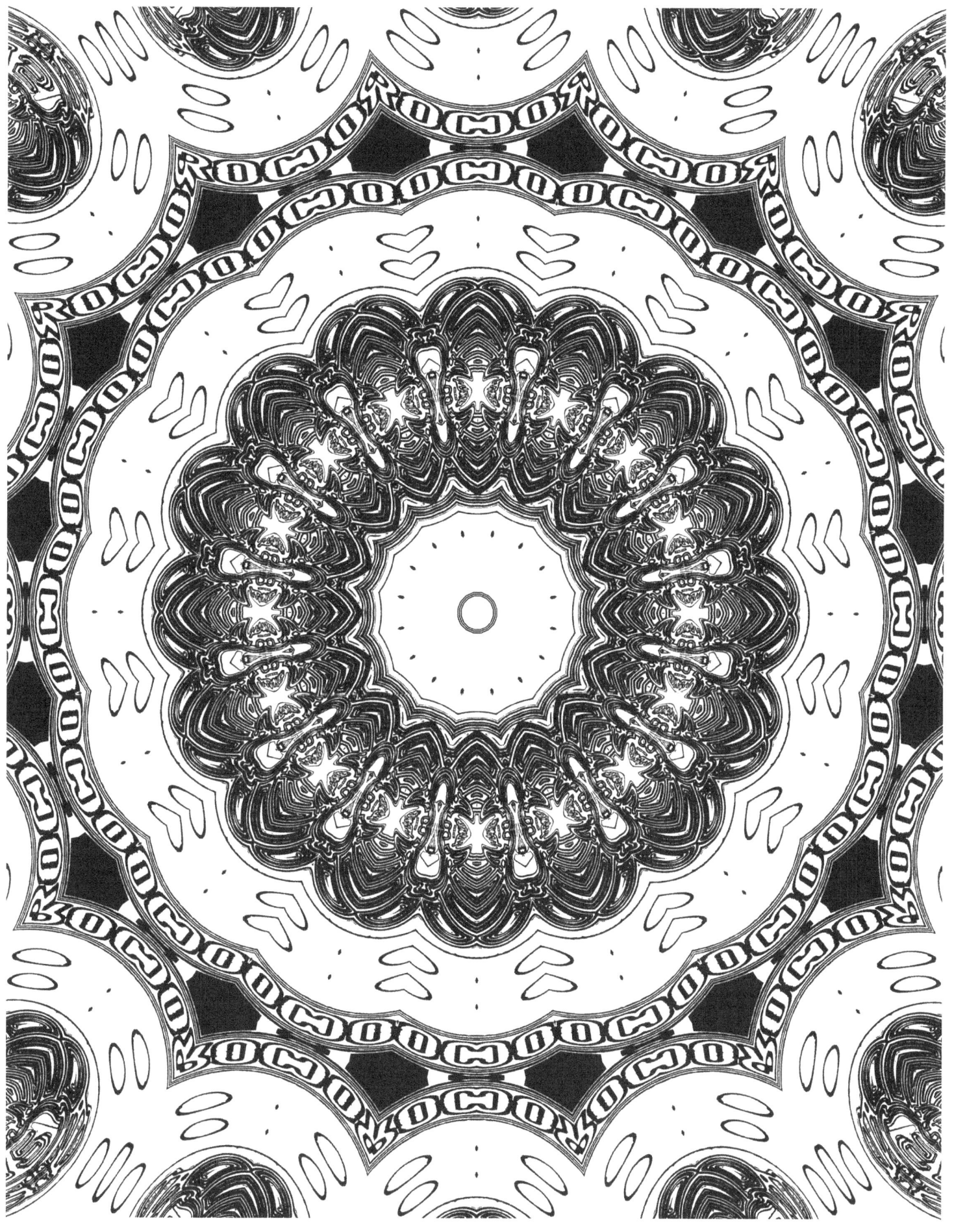

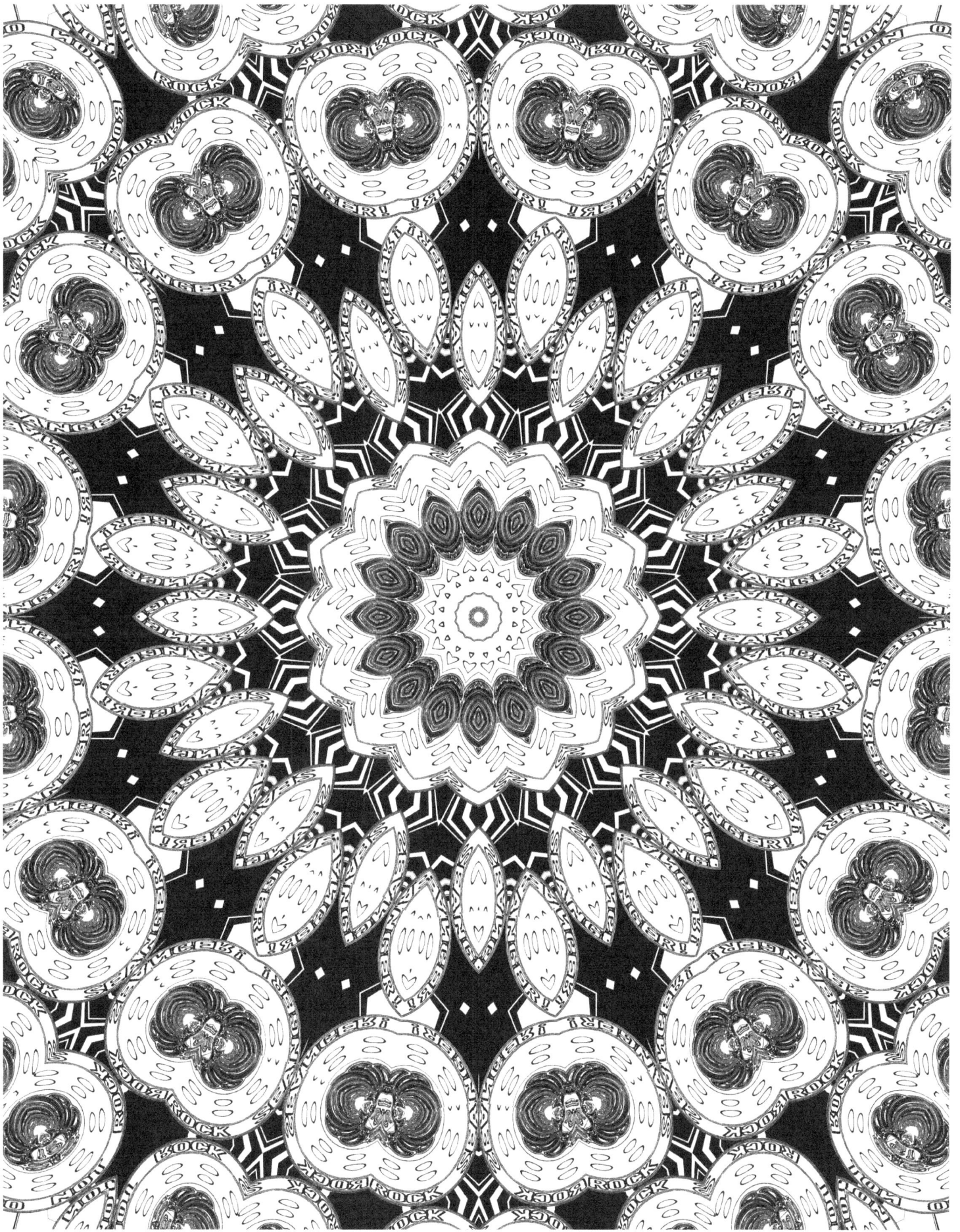

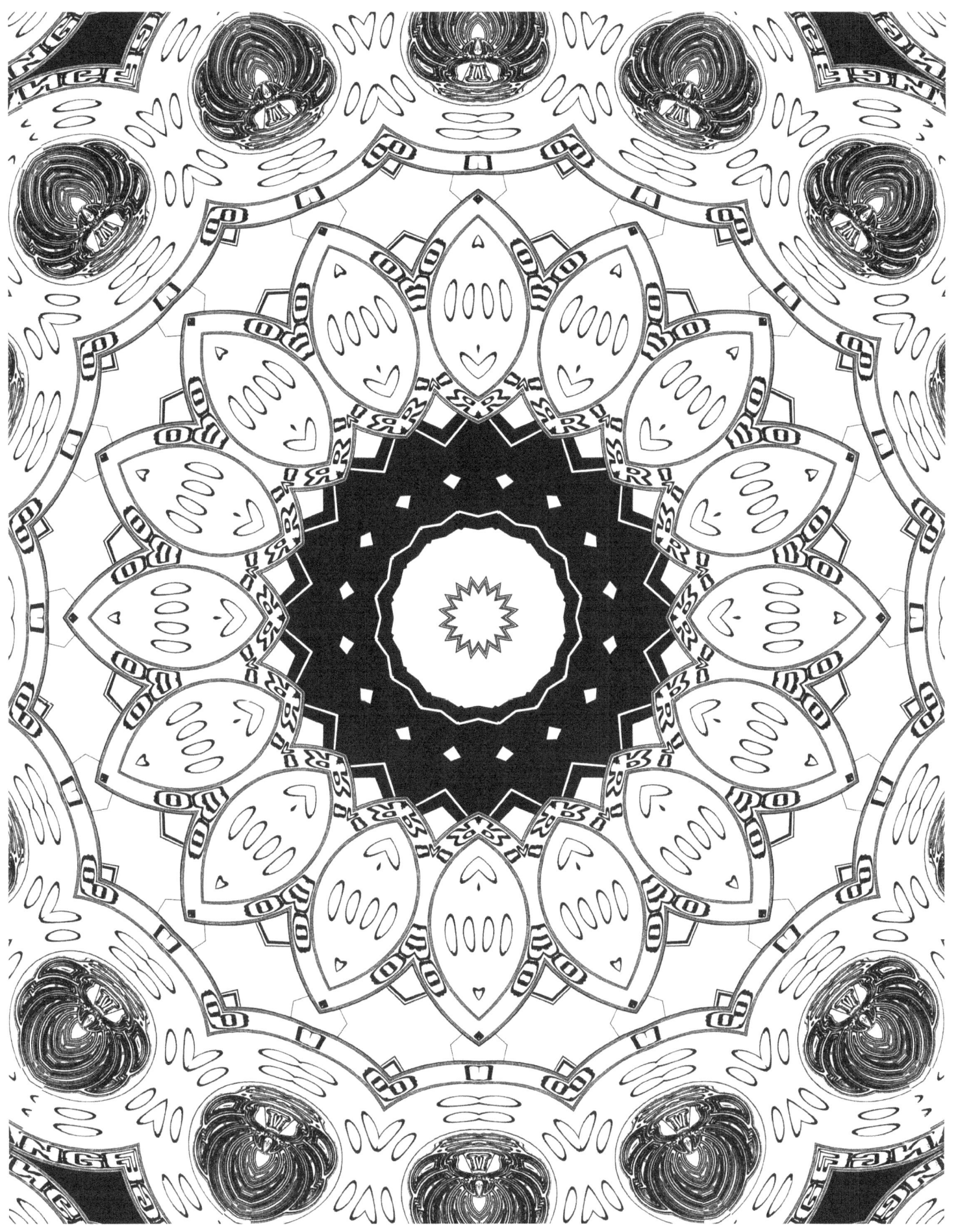

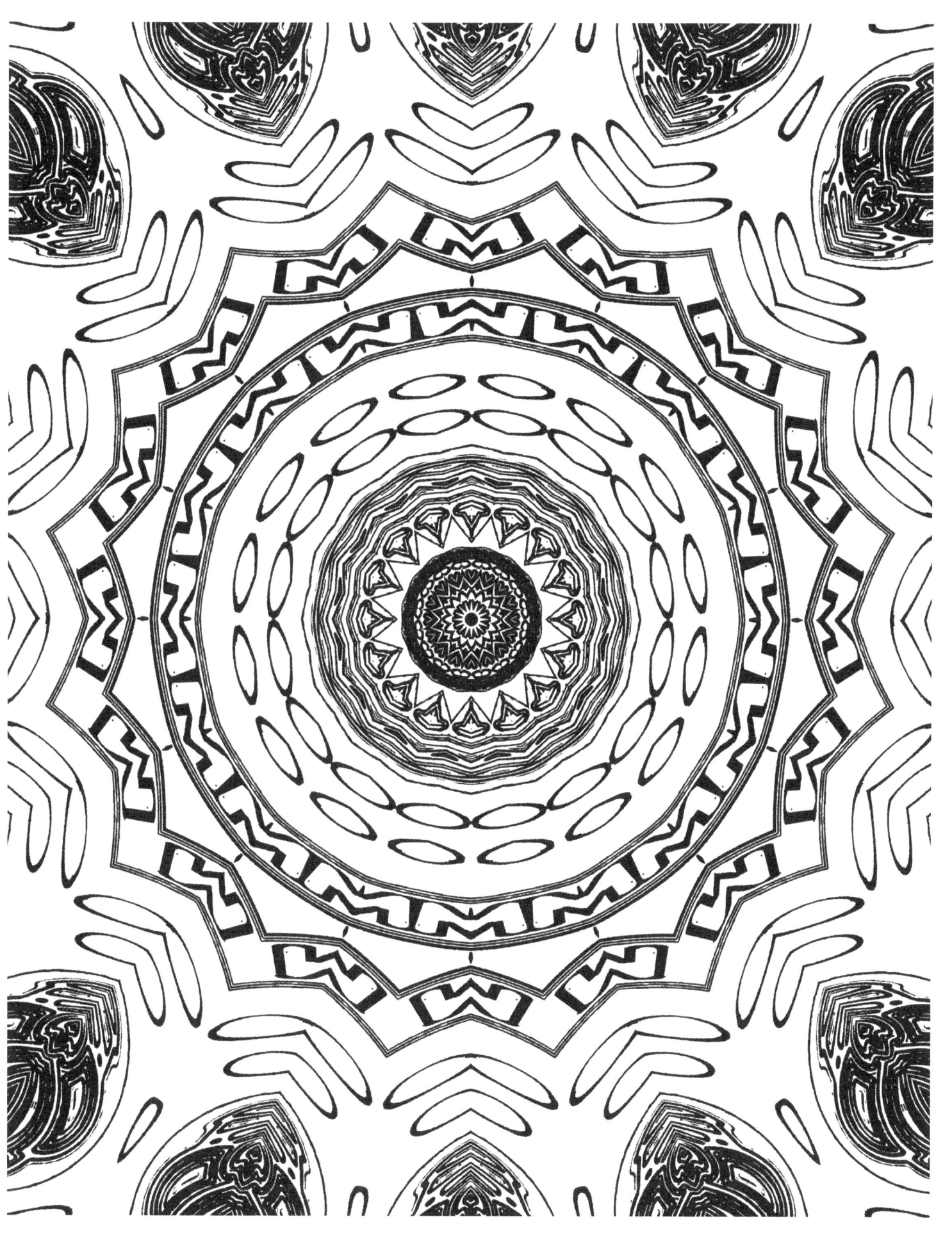

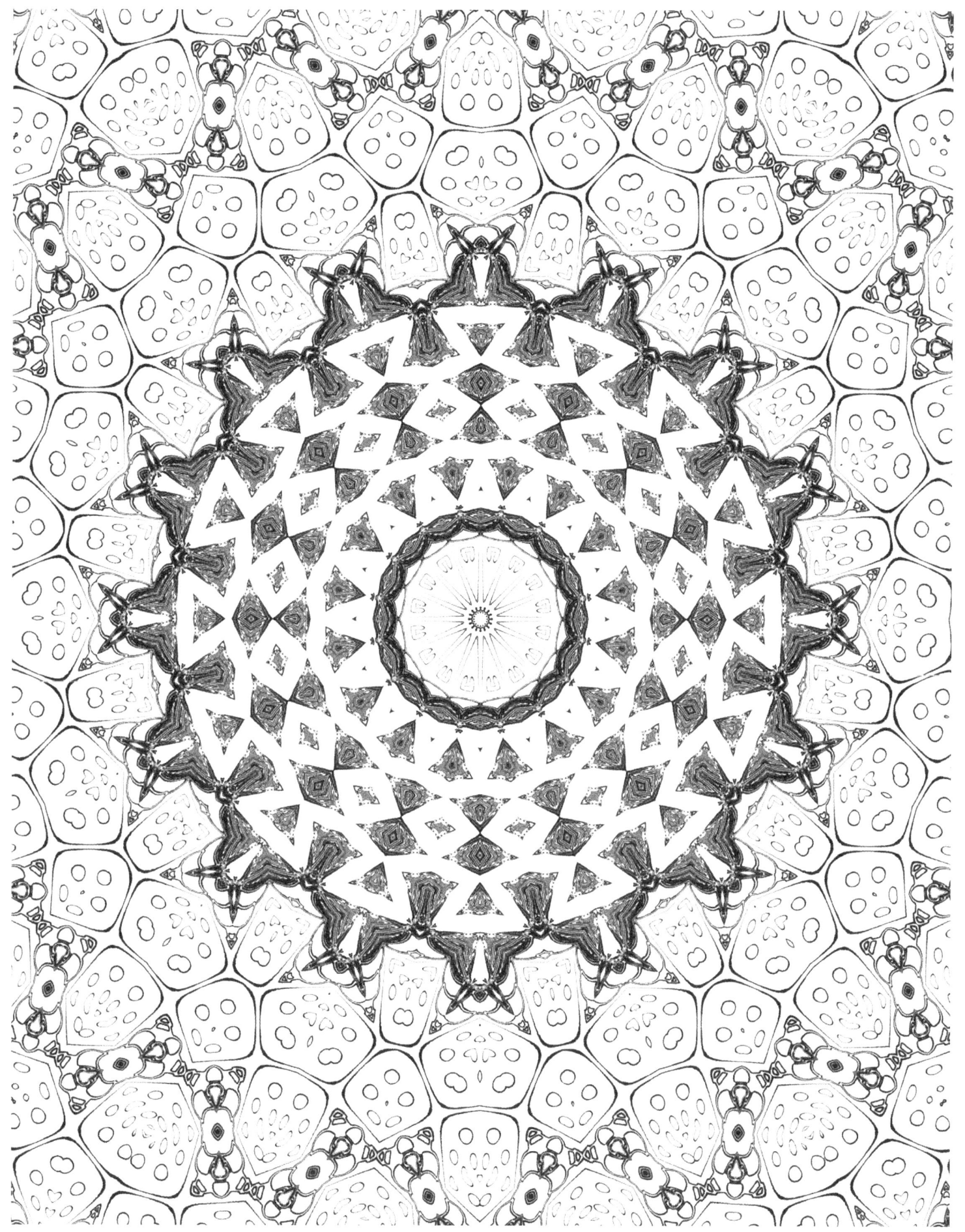

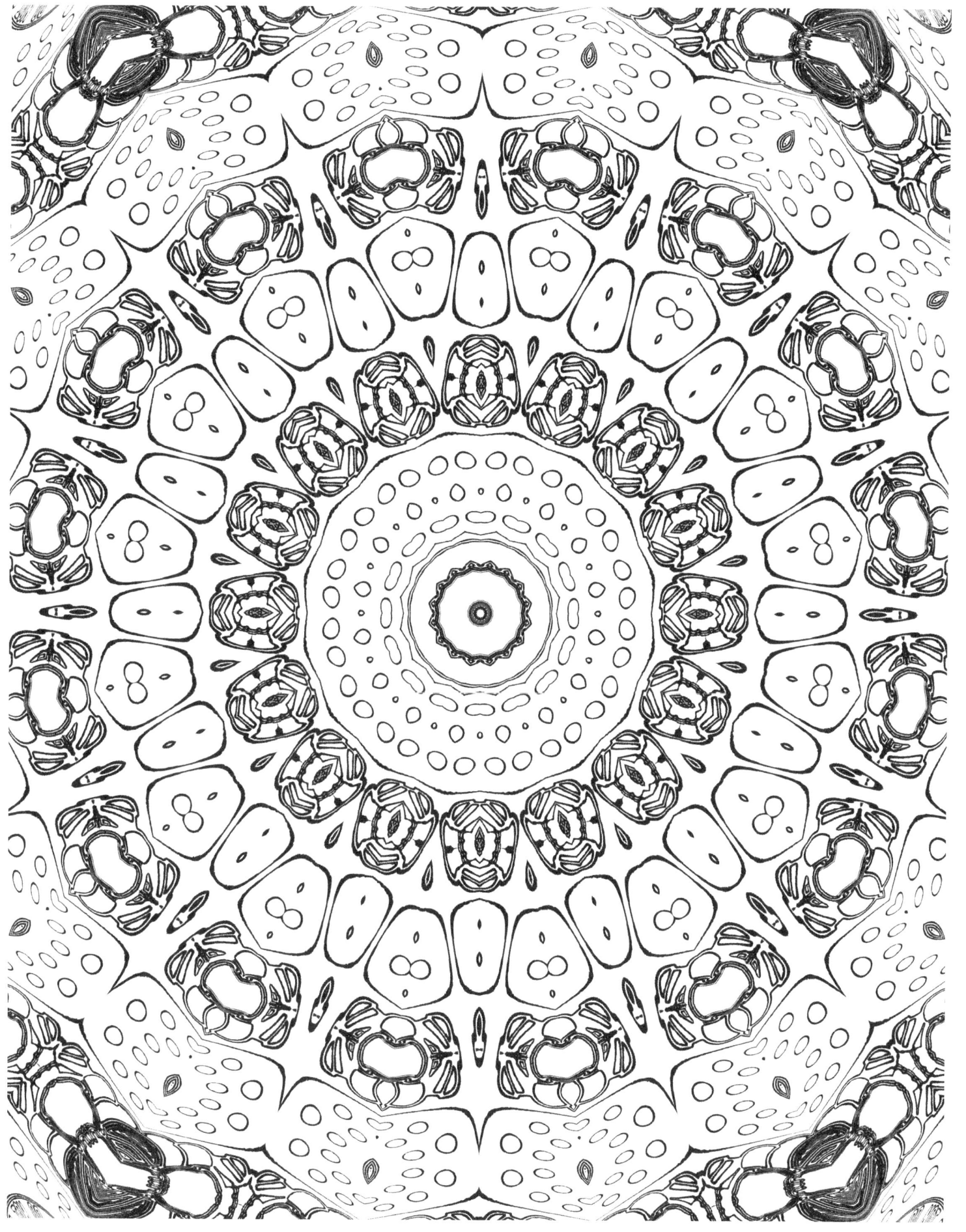

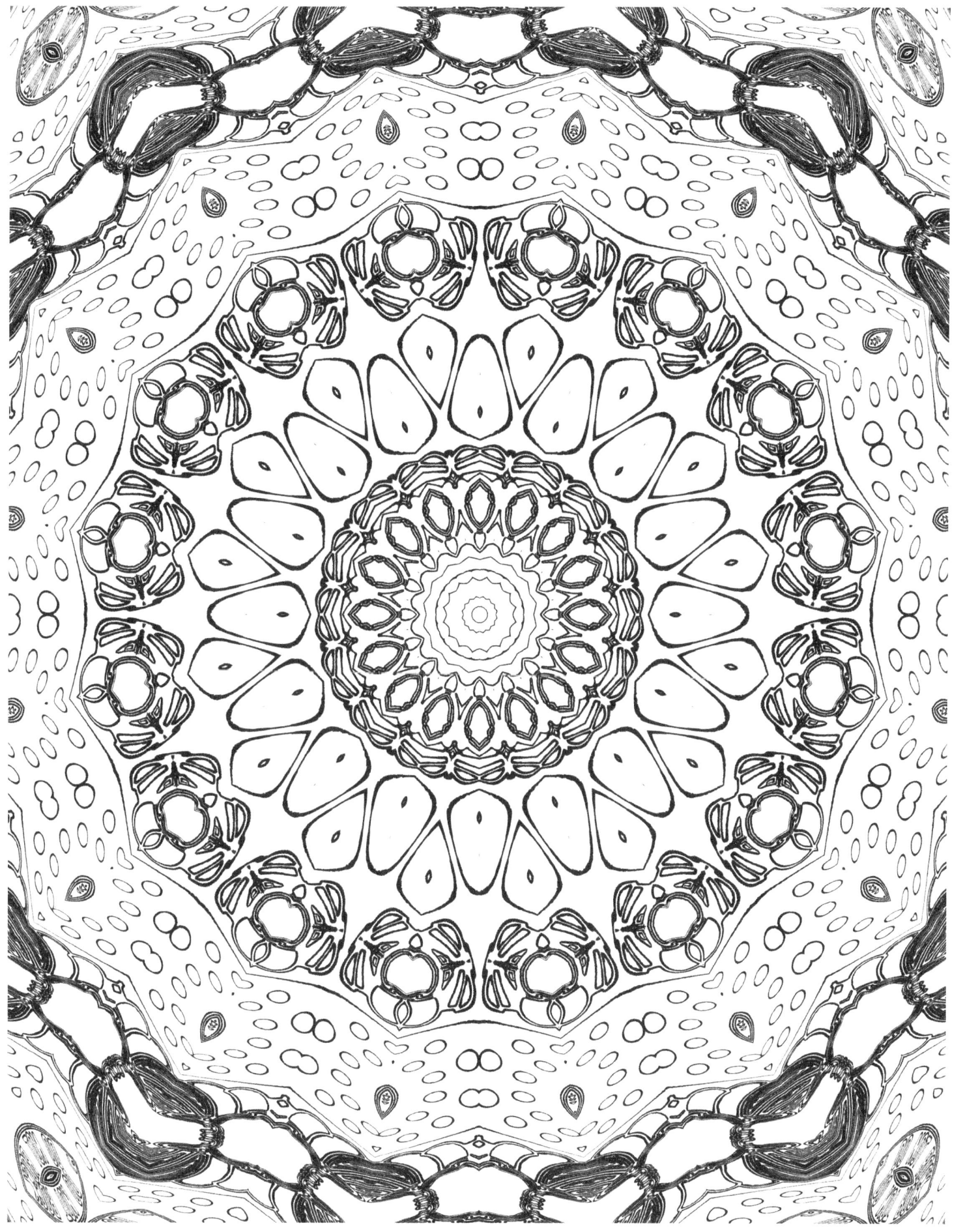

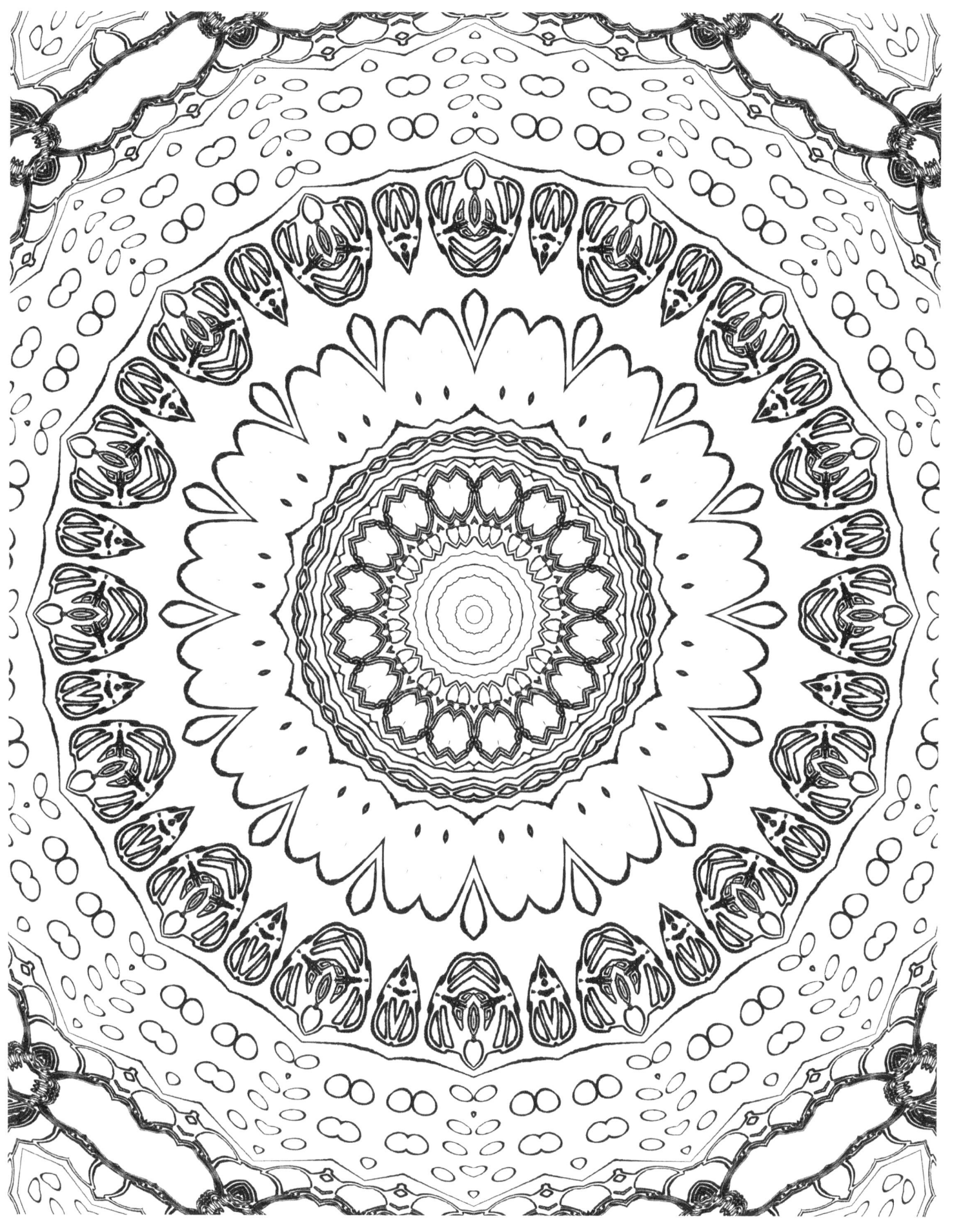

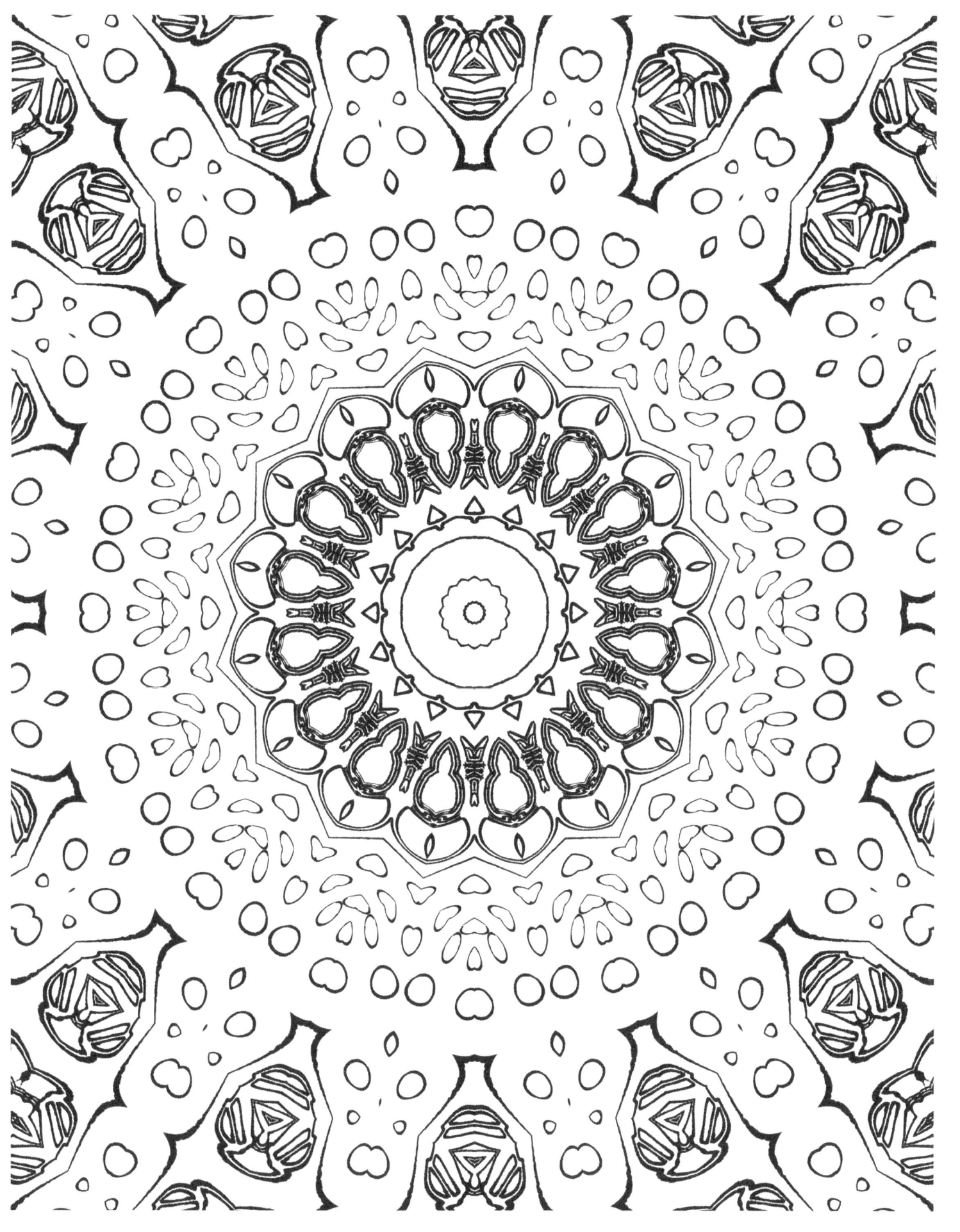

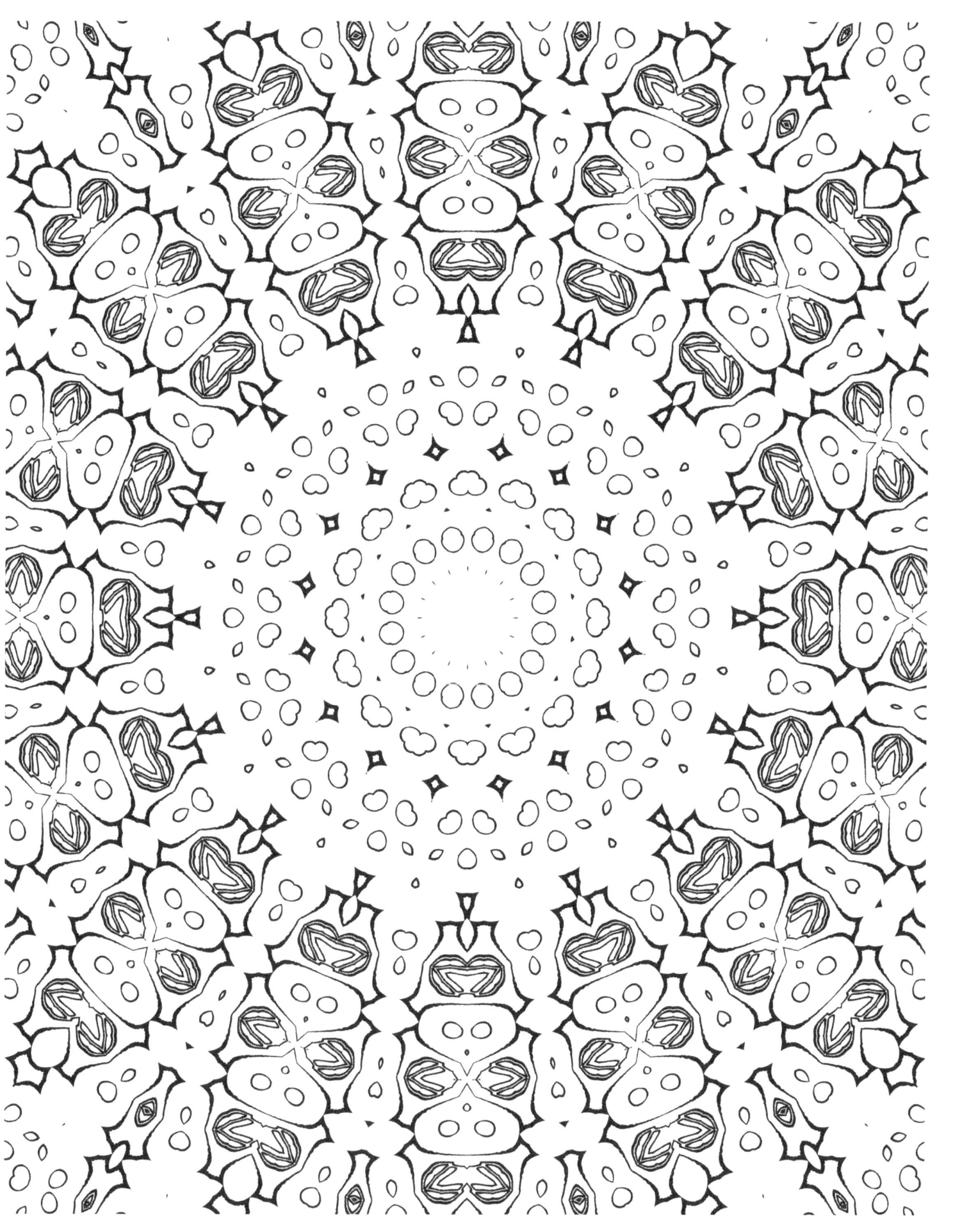

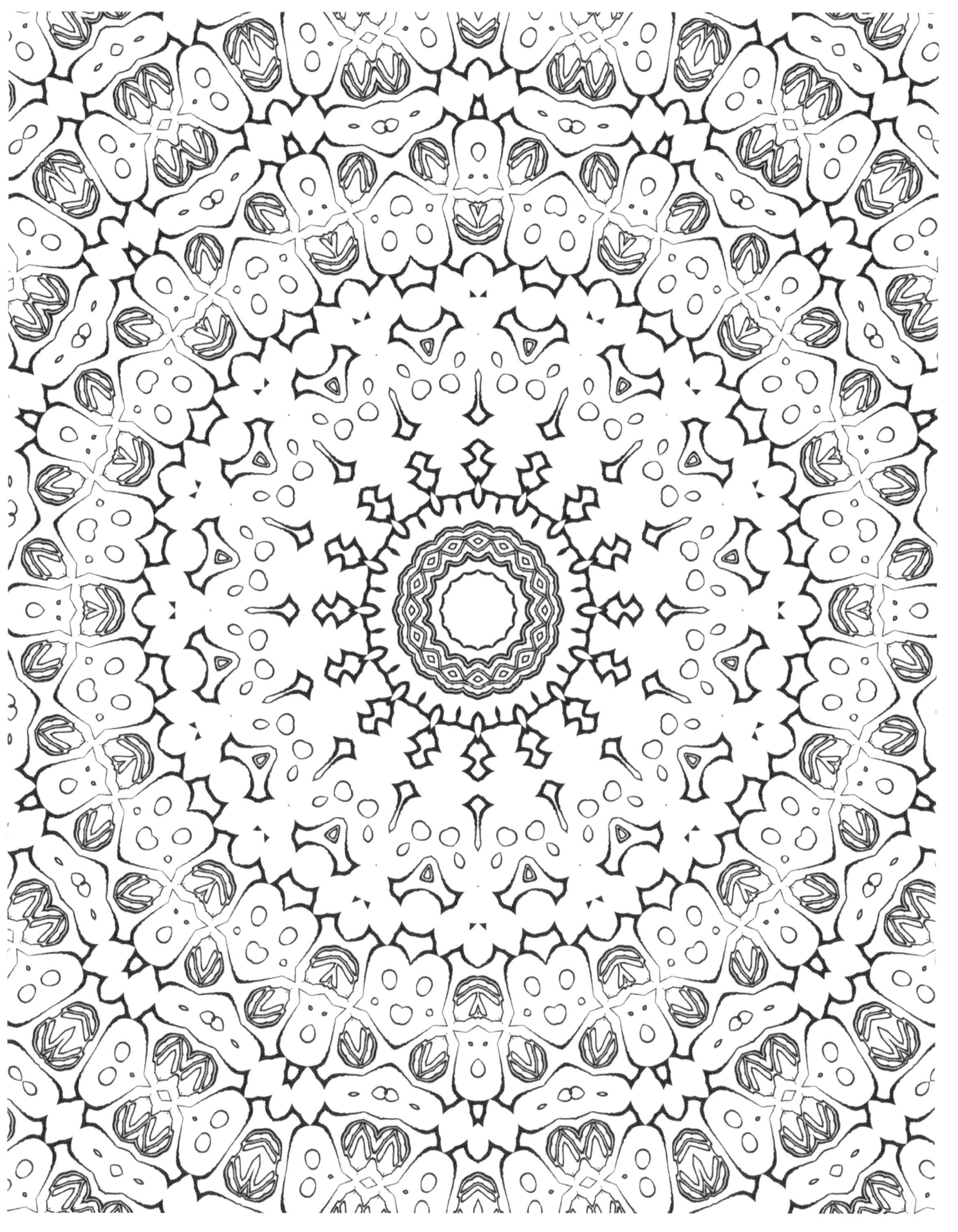

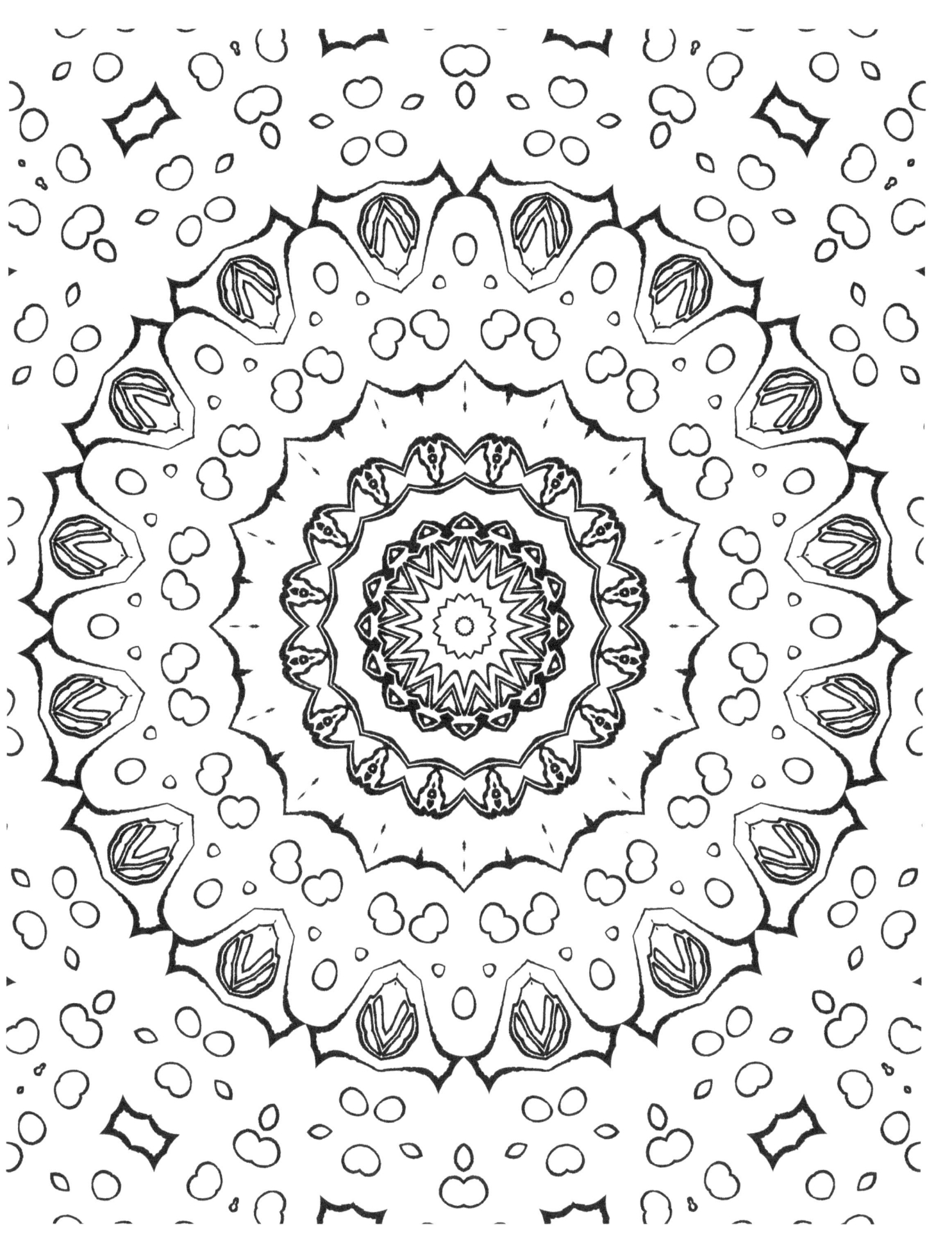

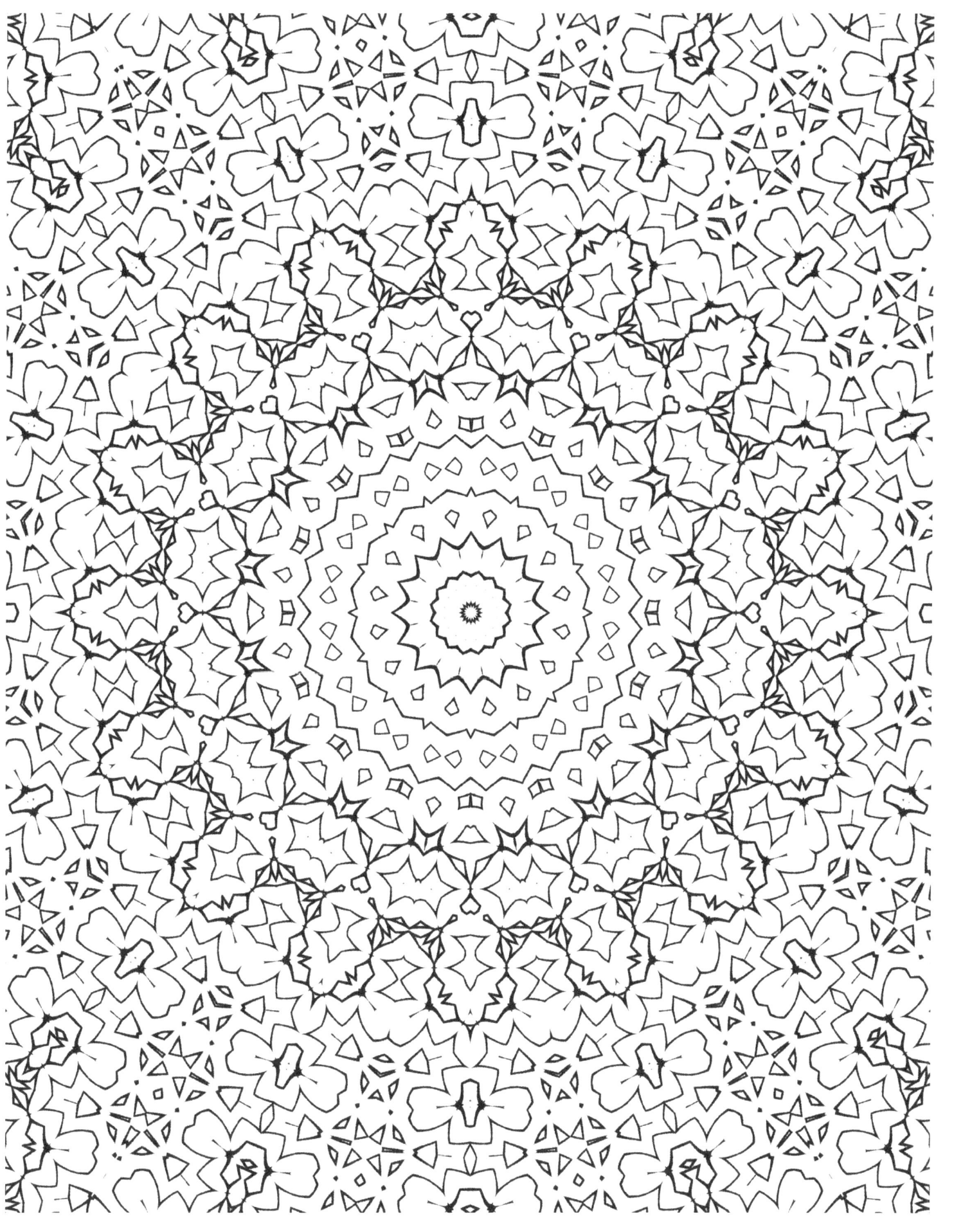

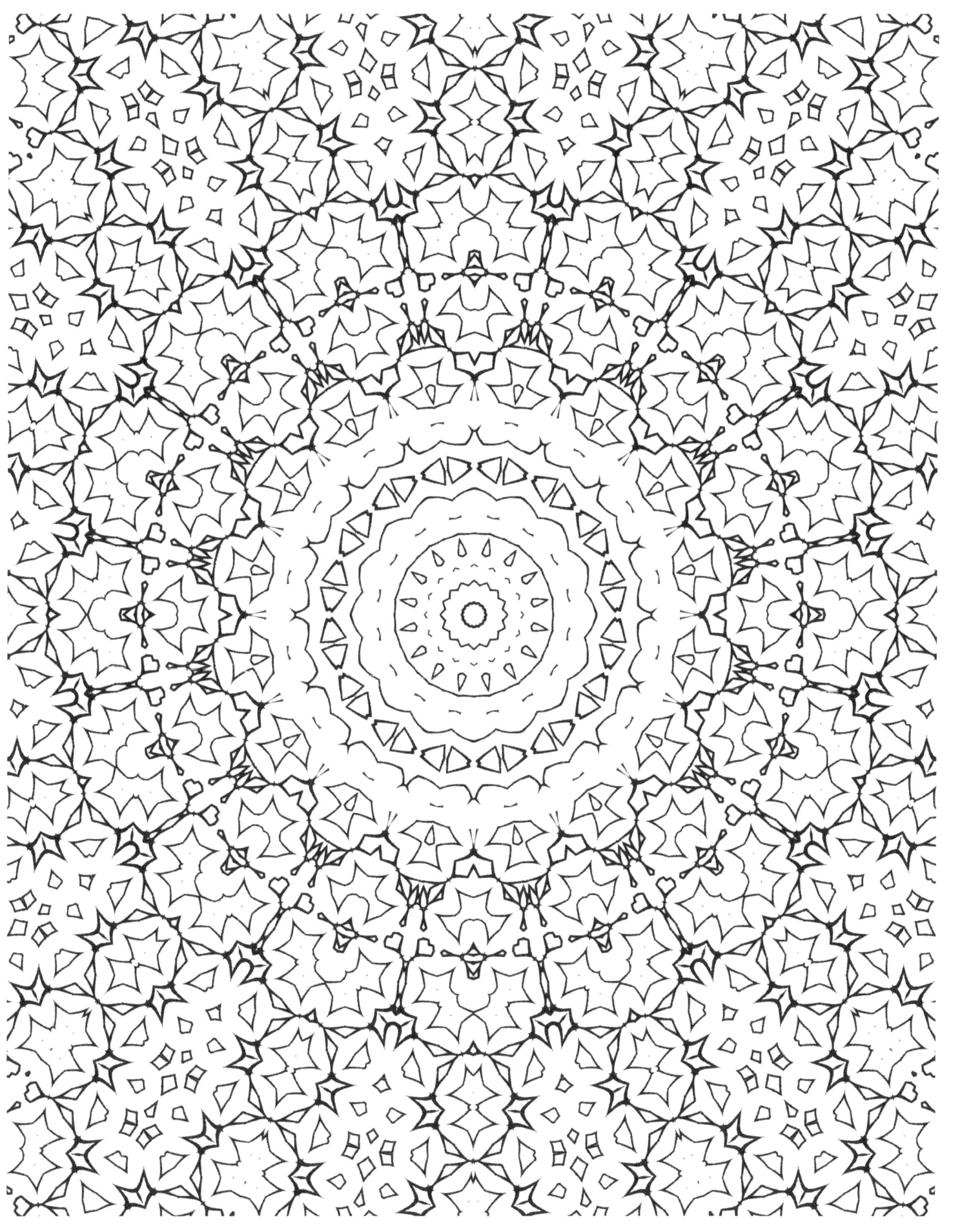

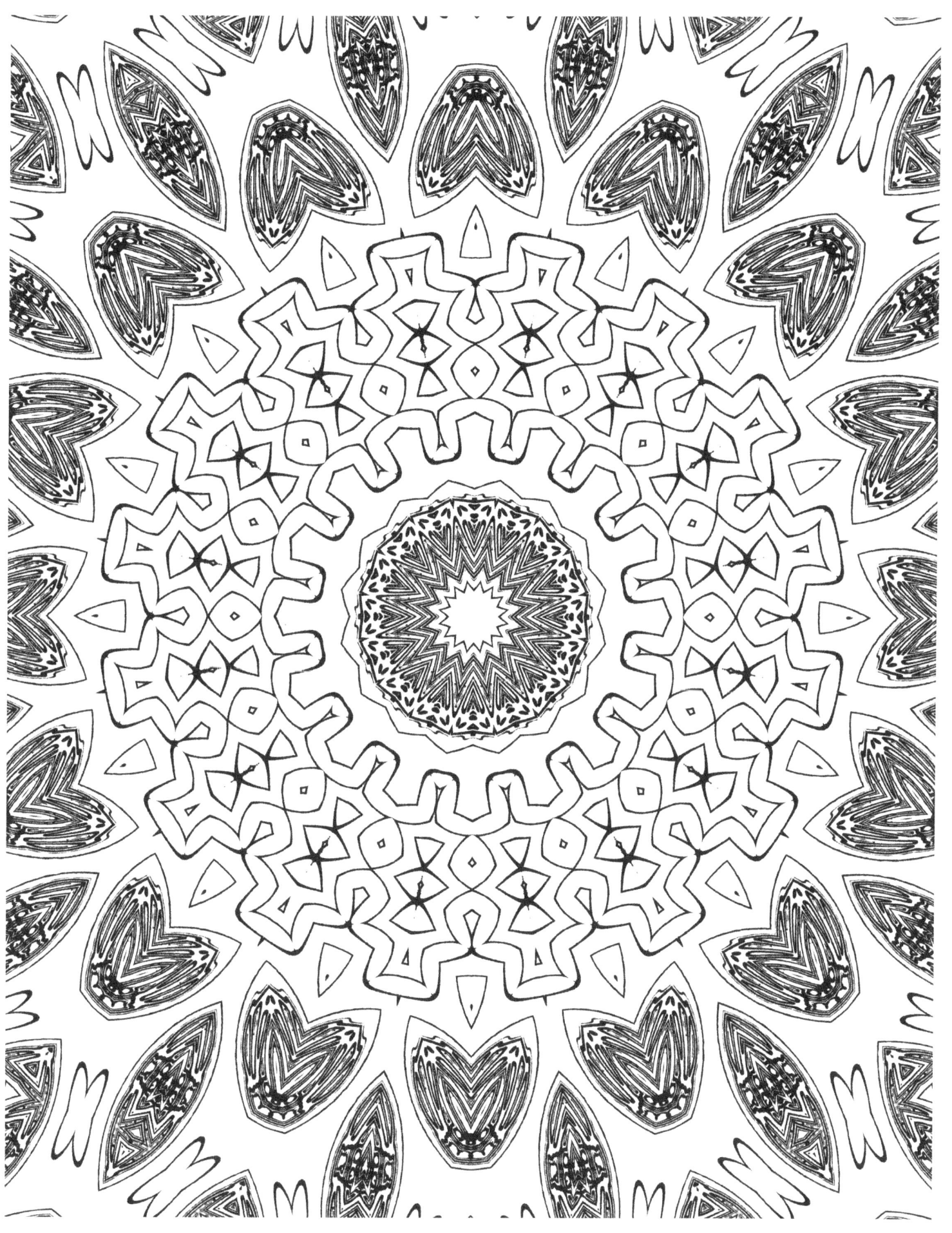

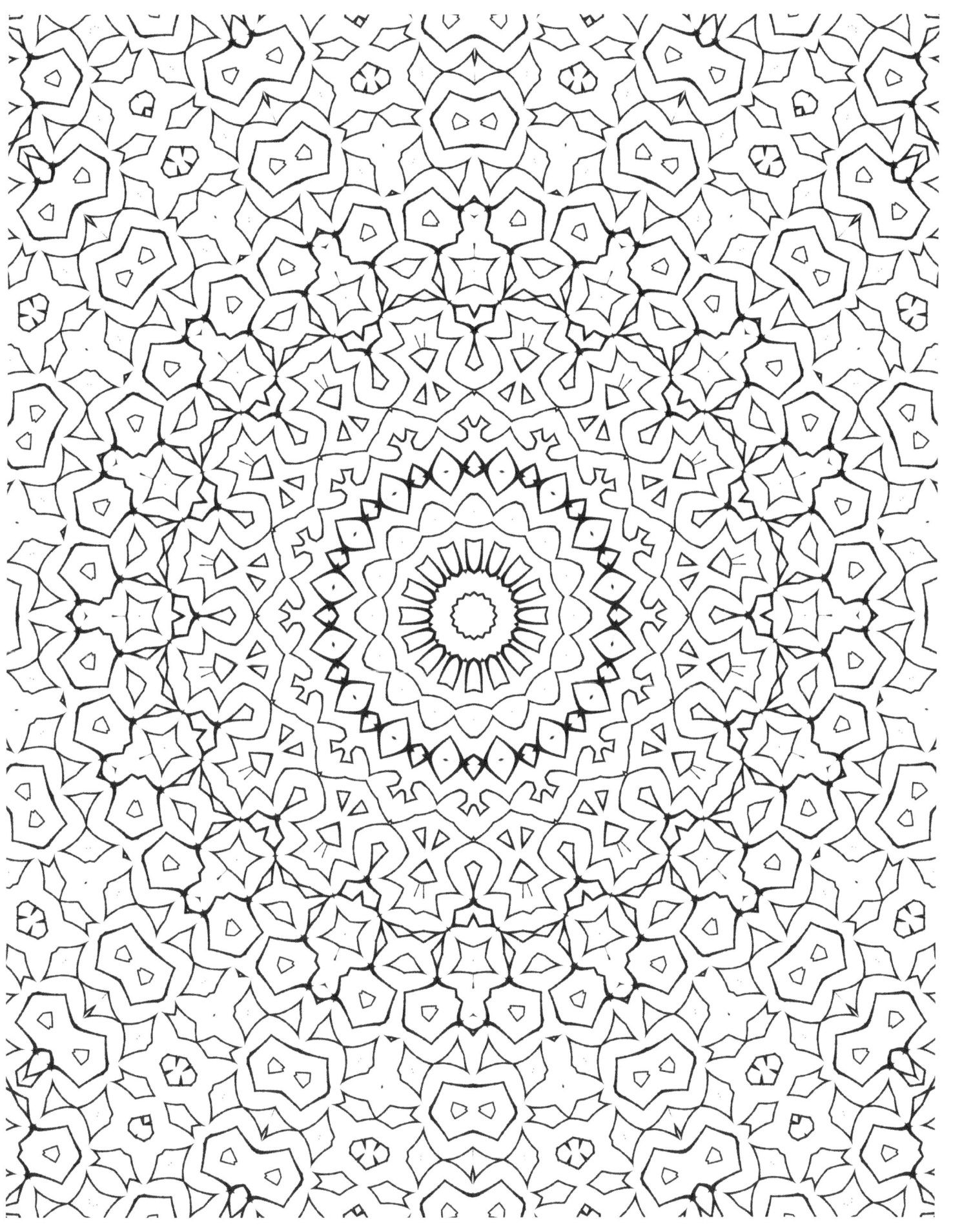

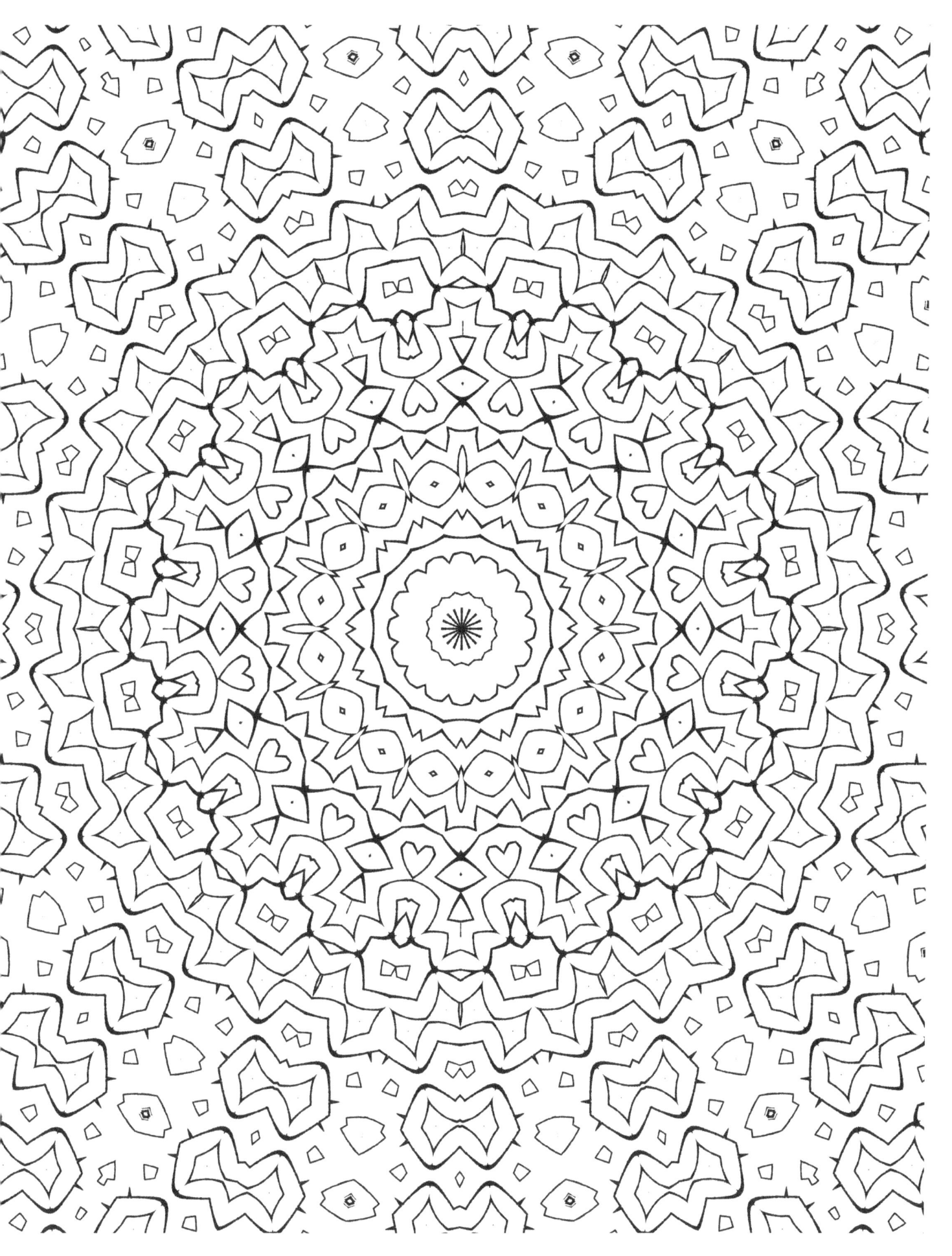

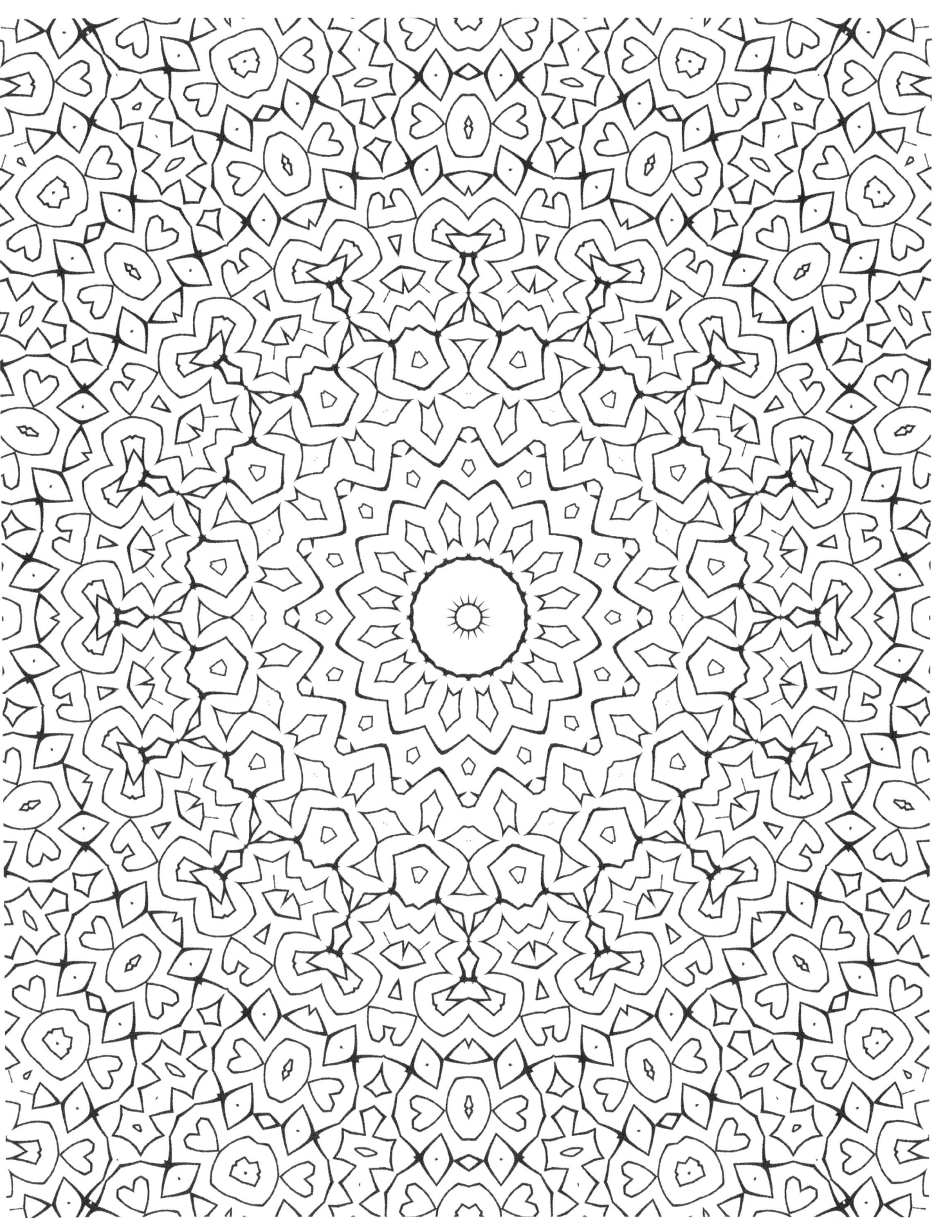

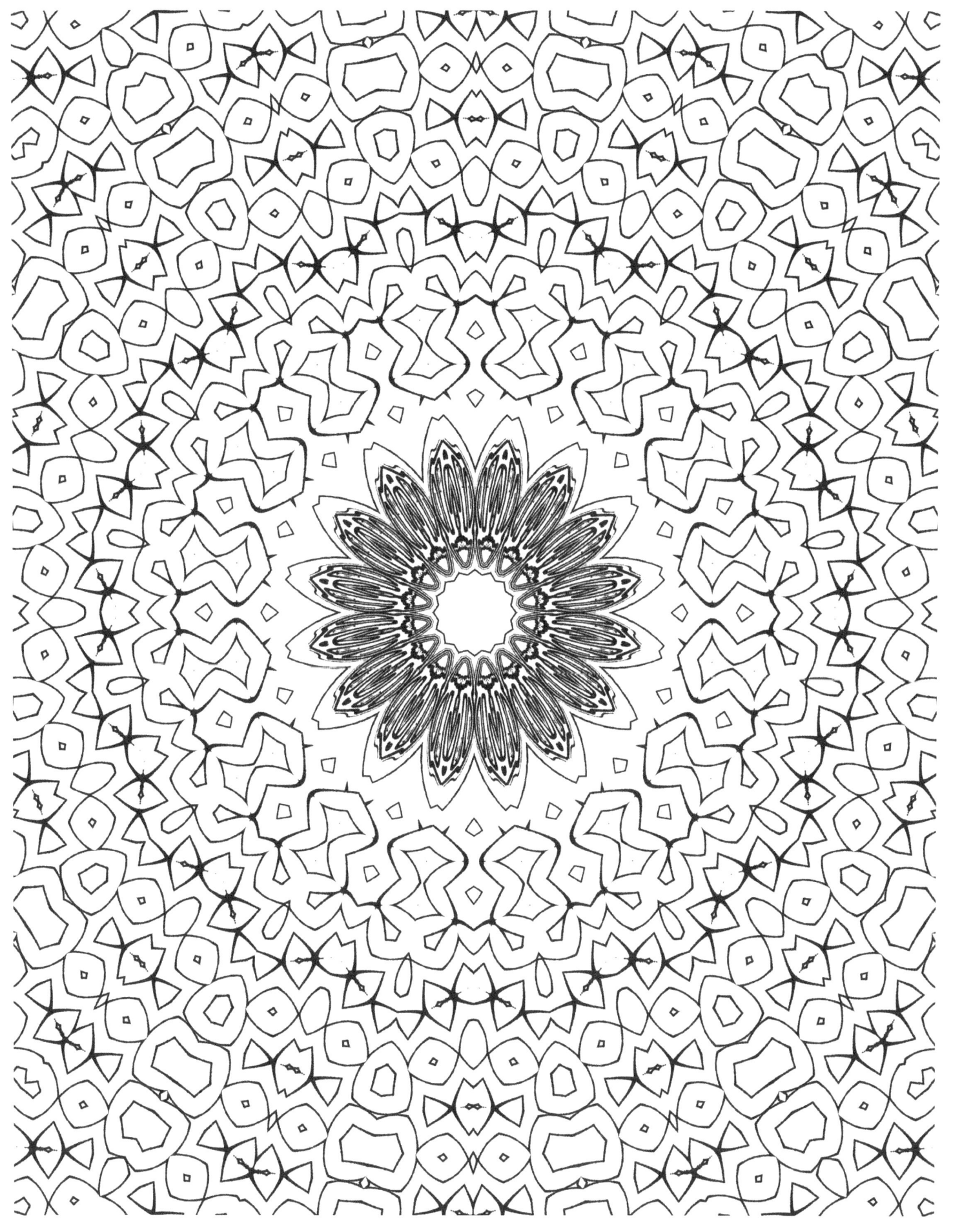

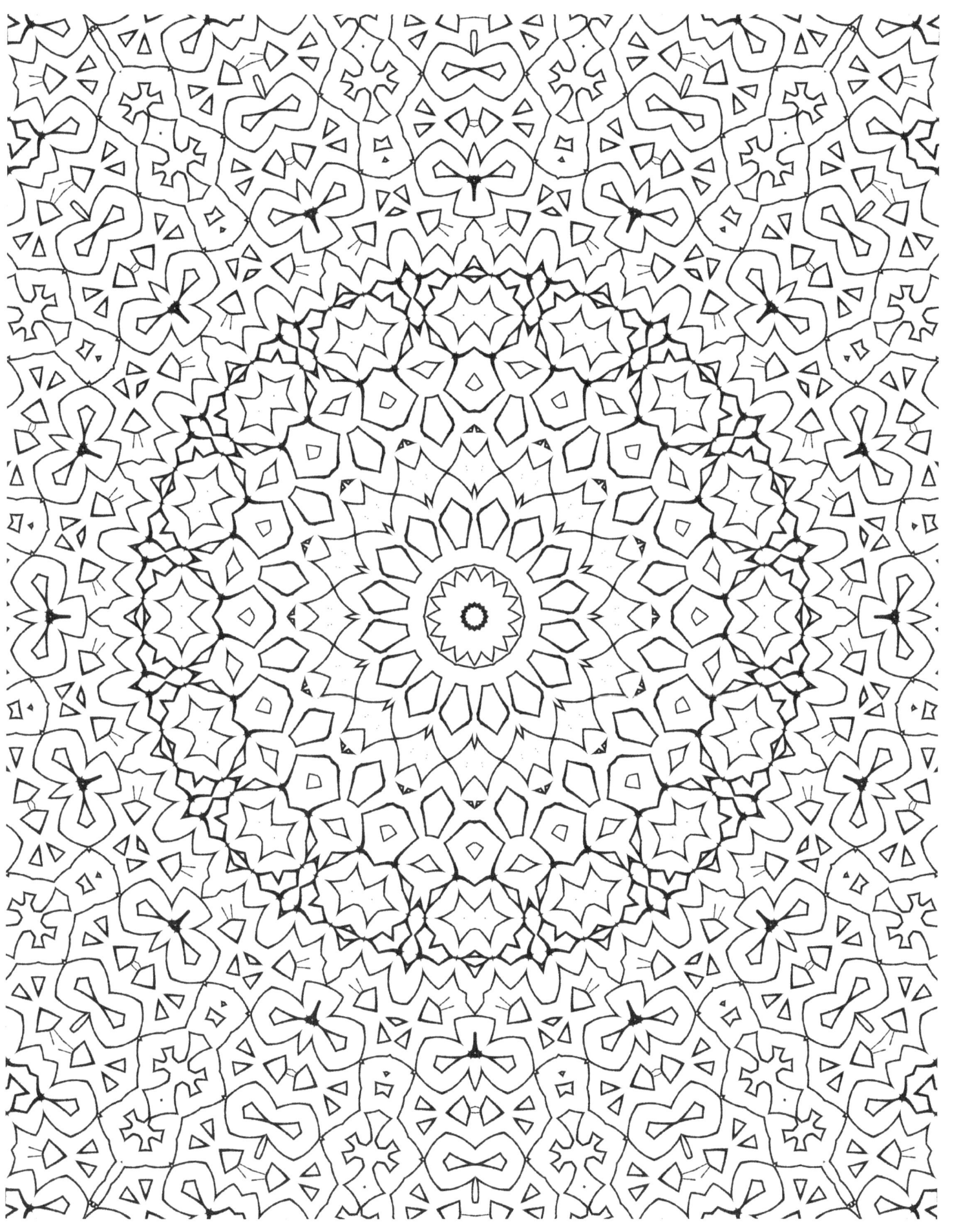

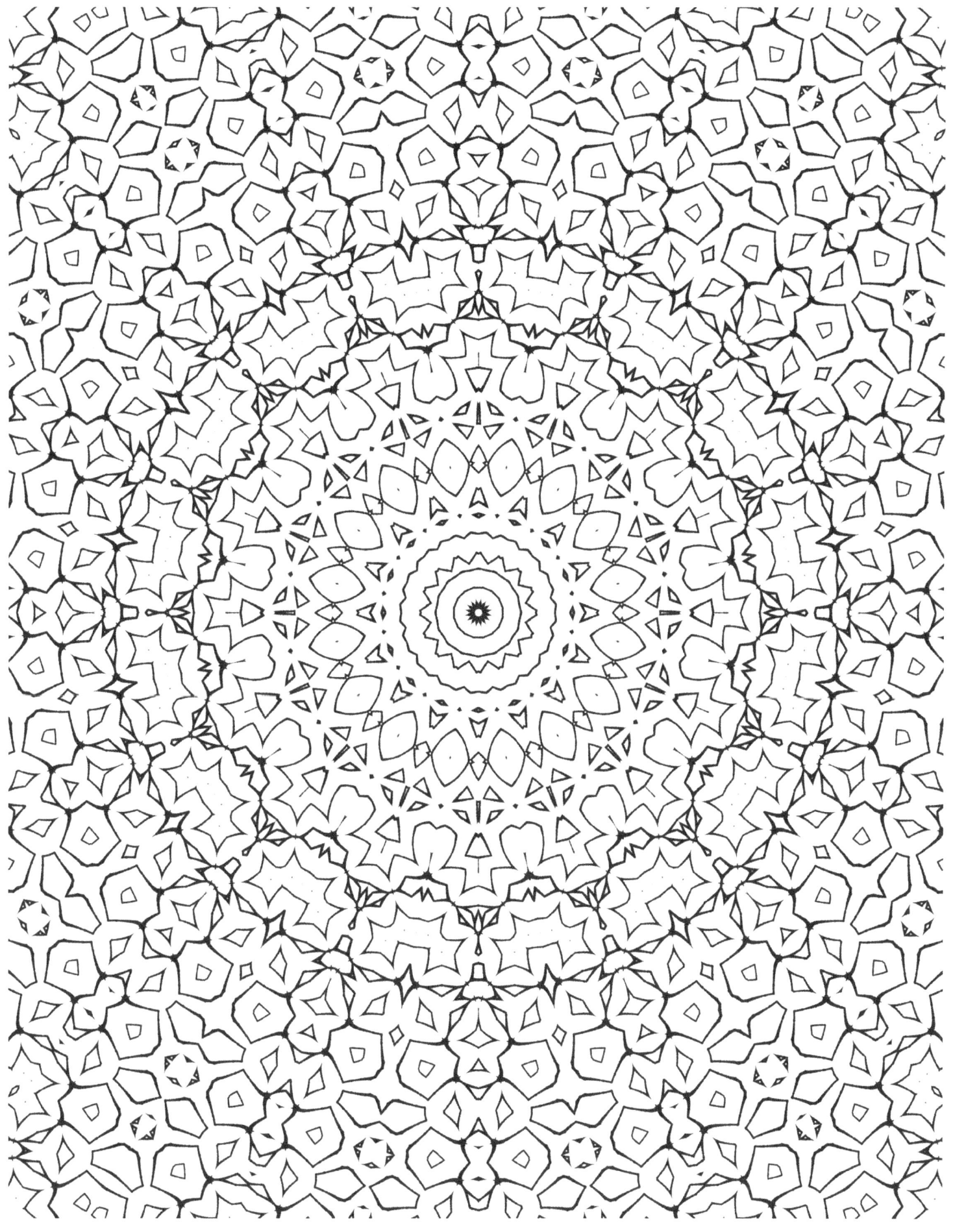

www.ingramcontent.com/pod-product-compliance
Lightning Source LLC
Chambersburg PA
CBHW080720190526
45169CB00006B/2452